No More Dodos

NO MORE DODOS

How Zoos Help Endangered Wildlife

Nicholas Nirgiotis and Theodore Nirgiotis

Lerner Publications Company • Minneapolis

To Georgia with love and thanks.
—NN

To my wife Andrea for all her love and support.
—TN

Our gratitude to our editor, Joelle Goldman, for her dedication and wise counsel.
—NN/TN

Library of Congress Cataloging-in-Publication Data

Nirgiotis, Nicholas.
  No More Dodos : how zoos help endangered wildlife / by Nicholas Nirgiotis and Theodore Nirgiotis.
    p. cm.
   Includes bibliographical references and index.
   Summary: Describes the efforts to save such animals as the black-footed ferret, the golden lion tamarin, and the California condor from extinction through programs designed to protect endangered species.
   ISBN 0-8225-2856-8 (alk. paper)
   1. Wildlife reintroduction—Juvenile literature. 2. Endangered species—Juvenile literature. 3. Zoos—Juvenile literature. 4. Wildlife conservation—Juvenile literature. [1. Wildlife conservation. 2. Endangered species. 3. Wildlife reintroduction.] I. Nirgiotis, Theodore. II. Title.
   QL83.4.N57 1996
   639.9'79—dc20   95-45972

Manufactured in the United States of America
1 2 3 4 5 6 – JR – 01 00 99 98 97 96

CONTENTS

"Dead as a Dodo"   *7*

1   A Home on the Range   *11*

2   The Zoos Go Wild   *23*

3   Operation Noah's Ark   *33*

4   The Frozen Zoo   *51*

5   A Planet in Crisis   *65*

6   The Return of the Natives   *83*

7   The Web of Life   *101*

Glossary   *106*

For Further Reading   *109*

Index   *110*

ROELANDT.
SAVERY FE 1626.

This portrait of a dodo was painted in 1626. Fifty years later the species was extinct.

"Dead as a Dodo"

We know what the dodo looked like only because a few of the people who saw it made paintings and drawings. And there are one or two dodo skeletons preserved in museums. Aside from that, nothing remains.

The paintings show a bird the size of a large turkey with a huge, hooked bill and short, yellow legs. It was found only on Mauritius, a small island in the middle of the Indian Ocean. Sadly, no one will ever be able to see a real dodo again, either in its natural home or in a zoo exhibit. What happened to the dodo?

No people lived on Mauritius until Portuguese sailors discovered the island in 1507. The sailors found thousands of dodos living there. The birds were tame. Since they had no natural enemies and food was plentiful on the ground, dodos didn't need to fly. Over many thousands of years of easy living, their wings had become useless. Because the birds offered no resistance when captured, the sailors named them *doudo,* which means "foolish" in Portuguese.

Sailors killed many of the helpless birds for their meat. But what doomed the dodo was the introduction of pigs and monkeys to the island by Portuguese settlers. Dodos had no defense against these foreign creatures that ate dodo eggs and any dodo chicks that managed to hatch. Settlers cultivated more and more of the island's fertile land, dramatically reducing the bird's

Steps to Extinction

Rare—a plant or animal species whose population is small and isolated. Not many of its members can be seen in the wild, but its population is stable.

Threatened or vulnerable—a plant or animal species that may be abundant in some areas, but that still faces serious dangers. It is likely to become endangered in the near future.

Endangered—a plant or animal species whose numbers have been reduced to such an extent that it is in immediate danger of becoming extinct. Such a species needs help from humans to survive.

Extinct—a plant or animal species that no longer exists. No individual members can be found alive anywhere.

The serval is common in Africa south of the Sahara Desert, but a population in the northern part of the continent is endangered.

habitat. By 1680 the dodo was extinct. In its place we had a new expression to remind us of its fate: "Dead as a dodo."

Extinction is a natural process that has occurred throughout the earth's history. Species either adapt to changing environmental conditions and survive, or they decline and are replaced by others. But humans are changing the environment too quickly for species to have time to adapt. Many species are becoming extinct, and the diversity of life on which humans and other species depend is collapsing.

Because of what happened to the dodo, we are aware of the power people have to destroy or to preserve the earth's species. And that awareness is being put to good use. With time running out for many species that share the earth with us, organizations dedicated to the preservation of wildlife and the environment have stepped up their efforts. They are working hard to save as many as possible of the animals facing the fate of the dodo.

Zoos stand at the forefront of the rescue operation. They are using exciting new ideas and the latest in technology to carry out their mission. They intend to prevent other species from vanishing as the dodo did. Their goal can be expressed in the motto, "No More Dodos!"

A black-footed ferret surveys the area around its burrow.

Chapter One

A HOME ON THE RANGE

The price on the masked stranger's head was high. Thousands of dollars would be paid to anyone who spotted the secretive night prowler with the dark eyes and the thick, powerful neck— no questions asked. But there was one catch. The stranger would have to be found alive and well and living in the wild.

The biologists who had set the reward were not looking for a bank robber. They were after the black-footed ferret, a small, sausage-shaped animal that stalks its prey at night on the Montana and Wyoming prairies. It was one of the most endangered mammals in North America, and scientists were desperately searching for any survivors that might still exist in the wild.

Black-footed ferrets are members of the weasel family. They are just 20 inches long, and they weigh about 2 pounds. They are slightly smaller than their closest wild relatives, the European polecat and the Siberian polecat. Domestic ferrets, descended from the European polecat, were once used to hunt rats and rabbits. They are often kept as pets.

Black-footed ferrets have long bodies that are ideal for moving quickly over brush-covered ground and through burrows. Their brown fur, trimmed with black on their feet and tail tip, helps them blend into their surroundings. They got the nickname "masked bandits of the prairies" because they seem to hide behind a black face mask. Black-footed ferrets live near prairie dog colonies because they feed almost exclusively on prairie dogs. The ferrets even make their homes in the burrows prairie dogs dig.

Once ferrets were common in western North America from Canada to northern Mexico. They managed to thrive in the wild, despite the coyotes, badgers, owls, and bobcats that hunted them. But the farmers and ranchers who settled the western prairies at the end of the nineteenth century proved to be far deadlier enemies.

Many western ranchers consider prairie dogs pests because they are grass eaters and compete for food with cattle and sheep. Also, any horse or cow that steps into a prairie dog burrow is likely to break a leg, and such an animal has to be destroyed. In 1914, the federal government stepped in to solve the prairie dog problem. A campaign to shoot, trap, and poison prairie dogs out of existence was begun.

The war against the prairie dog was a great success. By the early 1970s prairie dogs could be found in just two percent of their former habitat, and their population had shrunk to a tiny fraction of what it once had been. With their food supply gone, most black-footed ferrets had vanished as well.

On the Brink

When biologists realized the extent of the danger facing the ferrets, they decided to organize a rescue effort. The surest way to locate any ferrets remaining in the wild was to search close to existing prairie dog towns and to offer a reward to anyone who sighted a ferret and reported its location.

In 1981, there was a bit of luck. A rancher reported finding a small group of ferrets near Meeteetse, in northwestern Wyoming. There were a number of animals in this group, and

An Uneasy Alliance

Since black-footed ferrets depend on prairie dogs (shown above) for their diet and their shelter, the survival of prairie dog towns is critical to the ferret recovery program. But many landowners in the West consider prairie dogs to be destructive pests and continue to shoot and poison them.

The ferret recovery program must gain the cooperation of the people who own land around the recovery areas. To ensure the survival of the ferrets, these people must come to accept the presence of large prairie dog habitats. But many farmers and ranchers fear that ferret releases will bring about new federal regulations that restrict the way landowners control prairie dogs, even in areas that have no ferret population.

To quiet these fears, the ferrets are listed as "threatened," not "endangered." This designation allows landowners outside the ferret recovery area to control prairie dogs without fear of legal prosecution.

they seemed to be doing well. Hope grew that ferrets could be saved from extinction.

Up to that time, amazingly little was known about black-footed ferrets' behavior. So biologists immediately set to work learning how ferrets live in the wild, who their enemies are, what their mating habits are, and how they raise their young, or kits. The answers would help scientists develop a long-range plan for ferret survival.

Since ferrets are secretive loners that carry on their business mostly at night, it's extremely difficult to study them in the wild. They spend most of their time underground. When they do come aboveground, they move quickly. They are ever watchful, standing up straight on their hind legs to sniff the air for food and to look for signs of danger.

Biologists realized that disease or some other catastrophe could wipe out the entire species at once if these were the only ferrets left in the world. They decided that at the first hint of such a disaster they would be ready to remove some of the ferrets to a safe place. There, the ferrets would still have a chance to breed and increase in numbers. Their offspring could later be released in the wild.

To prepare for the eventual release of captive-bred ferrets, researchers studied the number of prairie dogs in different colonies in Montana and Wyoming and noted the distances between colonies. This information would be important when the time came to choose places to reintroduce the ferrets to the wild. If prairie dog colonies were too far apart, young ferrets might not be able to find food or mates when they left their mothers to live on their own.

In June 1985, there was bad news. An epidemic of sylvatic plague, a highly contagious infection transmitted by fleas, began killing the prairie dogs on which ferrets depended for their food. Soon after, the ferret population began to drop sharply.

In August, six ferrets were caught and moved to the Sybille Canyon Wildlife Research and Conservation facility in Wyoming. The ferrets were held in wire-mesh cages that allowed researchers to observe the animals without touching them. The cages had double-deck nest boxes so ferrets could retreat in daylight to sleep. These arrangements prevented stressing the ferrets.

Within days, one of the captives died of canine distemper, a deadly disease that spreads easily among ferrets. A few days later, all 6 ferrets were dead of distemper. Another group of 6 ferrets were quickly taken from the wild to the research facility, and soon after 12 more ferrets were captured. As far as anyone knew, these 18 were the total number of black-footed ferrets in existence.

Survival School

The ferret recovery program at Sybille got off to a slow start. After an anxious year, the ferrets finally began to breed. Researchers used video cameras to tape the ferrets' behavior. They were careful to maintain proper lighting conditions to fit the ferrets' nocturnal habits. These studies of ferret behavior helped scientists determine how many ferrets to reintroduce to the wild at one time, and whether to do it in stages or all at once.

As the studies continued, the researchers realized that if the ferrets remained in captivity too long, they would lose the instinct to escape predators. They began to develop a series of training programs, as well as release and monitoring techniques. The biologists tested their training programs on Siberian polecats. These animals are close relatives of the black-footed ferret, but they are not endangered.

By 1991, just six years after the captive breeding program started, the ferret population at the facility had increased from 18 to nearly 250. The population was large enough to begin a reintroduction program. The site chosen for the ferrets' new home was Shirley Basin in southeastern Wyoming.

Before the ferrets could be released, they had to be trained to survive in the wild. They were gradually weaned from food provided by people, and they were encouraged to develop ferret social skills so that they could find mates. Males were placed in cages with females when the females were in estrus, or ready to mate. Males thus learned the proper time for mating. Contact with humans was kept to a minimum, because tame animals would be helpless on their own in the wild.

Ferrets usually begin to explore their environment when they are five to six weeks old. So the kits were placed in special cages that had, in addition to the nest box, a box of tunneling material. The arrangement in each cage was changed weekly to help the growing kits develop the hunting skills they would need when they encountered prairie dogs. Prairie dog burrows are complicated systems of tunnels, chambers, and escape routes. Changing the tunnel arrangement gave the ferrets experience in dealing with this complexity.

A ferret looking for food has to locate a prairie dog burrow, dig its way into the prey's burrow, make the kill, and carry the prairie dog out of the burrow. Prairie dogs have sharp teeth and claws, and they fight back. Ferrets never have an easy time getting their dinner. So a small prairie dog town was set up in the captive breeding area to familiarize the ferrets with the homes of their prey.

Biologists constructed decoys that resembled predators to

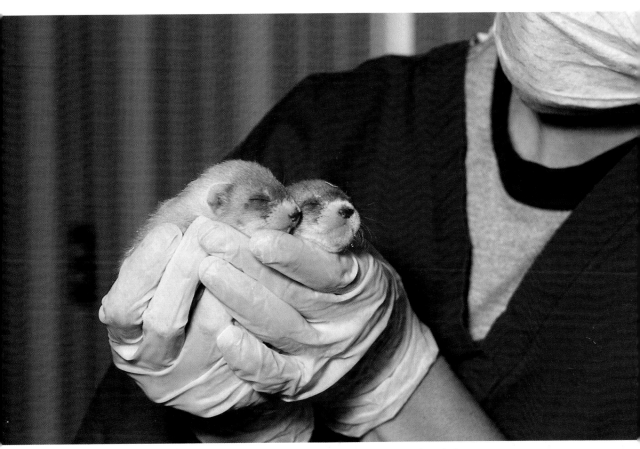

Researchers take precautions to ensure that captive-bred ferrets remain disease-free.

teach the kits how to detect their enemies. A stuffed great horned owl suspended from the ceiling on a fishing line was made to swoop toward ferret kits to teach them to be wary of flying predators. If the kits didn't dive into their holes quickly enough, they were shot with rubber bands. The most effective decoy in these training sessions was a robotic badger. This was

Tracking Wild Animals by Radio

Radio telemetry is a tool used by scientists to gather information about animals they cannot observe directly. The animal to be studied is captured and fitted with a radio collar or a tiny implanted transmitter, then released. The transmitter emits radio pulses or beeps that can be picked up on a radio receiver or meter. The receiving equipment can determine the direction and distance from which the signal is coming. By recording changes in the readings, scientists can pinpoint the movements of the animal they are tracking.

Recent technological advances in radio telemetry have also made it possible to measure an animal's breathing rate or tell when it is ready to mate. Transmitters have been designed that can produce a variety of different radio signals. Each transmitter can be set to a specific frequency that is distinct from others used in the same study. Scientists studying small groups of animals can use these special transmitters to tell which particular animal's signal they are receiving.

Portable telemetry gear is used to track red wolves in Alligator River National Wildlife Refuge in North Carolina.

made by placing a stuffed badger on a radio-controlled toy truck. As the badger raced toward ferret kits, rubber bands were shot at the ferrets. This drove home the point that badgers are dangerous and should be avoided.

Back on the Prairie

When biologists began releasing ferrets at Shirley Basin in the autumn of 1991, the animals were fitted with radio collars. This allowed field-workers to track the ferrets. The tiny transmitter attached to the collar of each released animal broadcast a radio signal. The signals were picked up at monitoring stations equipped with antennas and electronic receivers. Most of the monitoring took place at night, when the ferrets were active.

Field-workers used telemetry equipment at several separate tracking stations to pinpoint the location of each ferret, track its movements, and mark the prairie dog burrow in which it had decided to make its home. They knew that a particular ferret had died if its collar's signal didn't move for an extended period of time. They could tell if the ferrets were extending their territories from one prairie dog town to another. Monitoring also let trackers follow the activities of the animals during the spring breeding season.

Occasionally a ferret's radio signal disappeared for a few days. Sometimes this happened because the ferret was deep inside a prairie dog burrow and its radio pulse could not be detected. At other times a signal disappeared because the animal had strayed out of range of the receivers and was wandering aboveground on the prairie. If researchers were lucky enough to find the missing ferret, they set a wire-mesh trap to catch the fugitive and return it to the release site.

Sometimes the ferrets were observed visually, using a technique called spotlighting. Researchers roamed the prairie at night with spotlights, watching for "eyeshine," or light reflected from a ferret's eyes. In this way workers could directly monitor the location and aboveground activities of individual ferrets.

The black-footed ferret recovery program is a long-term

Zoo breeding programs are the only hope of keeping the black-footed ferret from becoming extinct.

project. So far, results have been encouraging, but it's too soon to be certain of the final outcome. A number of the released ferrets have disappeared and are assumed to be dead. Others are known to have been killed by badgers or coyotes. But every year a few more ferrets are ranging free in their natural prairie habitat. There's hope that the corner has been turned in the battle for their survival.

A second black-footed ferret reintroduction site, in Badlands National Park, South Dakota, was first used in 1994. There are plans to add another site in Wyoming and one in Montana. These will be followed by several others, until a total of 1,500 breeding animals are living at 10 widely separated locations. This will ensure that an epidemic in one location will not affect the entire species. Biologists inoculate the ferrets against canine distemper before releasing them, but the threat of disease will remain. Captive populations will be maintained to keep enough animals available to restock colonies if needed.

Several zoos have followed the black-footed ferret restoration project with interest. They have started breeding programs of their own. Ferrets have been sent to zoos in Omaha, Toronto, Louisville, Phoenix, and Washington, D.C. This cooperation among zoos is in keeping with the important new mission that zoos have assumed. With extinction threatening thousands of animal species, the zoos have become the front line in the struggle to save our precious wildlife.

At one time, zoos were organized only for the convenience of zoogoers. Modern zoos also consider the animals' preferences.

Chapter Two

THE ZOOS GO WILD

The small lowland gorilla was just three years old when he was caught by poachers, people who illegally kill or capture wild animals. He was taken away from his mother and out of his African rain forest home. Few gorillas that age could survive such an ordeal, but this one was lucky. Soon after his capture in 1961, an animal trader sold him to Zoo Atlanta. He spent the next 27 years of his life alone in an indoor cage. Zoo personnel named him Willie B. after William B. Hartsfield, the mayor of Atlanta.

Willie's keepers wanted him to be happy. They hung an old tire from a wall of his cage and put a television set in one corner. They hoped these toys would keep Willie from being bored. But the tire and the television set were hardly the playthings a growing gorilla needed.

By age 12, Willie had grown into a magnificent 460-pound, 6-foot-tall silverback, a mature male with a distinguishing streak of silver hair on his back. His broad chest and powerful arms made people think of King Kong. They crowded in front of his cage to see him.

Gorillas are gentle, shy creatures, despite their size and fearsome appearance. But confinement in a cramped cage and lack of exercise had made Willie restless and bad-tempered. He grew fat and lazy, paced in his cage, and ignored visitors. His cage was a real prison, and Willie B. was a very unhappy gorilla.

Where Zoos Get Animals

In the past, when zoos needed a particular animal, they would contact an animal dealer. The dealer then arranged for a field expedition to capture the animal. Modern zoos rarely do this. Most countries restrict the export of wildlife because overhunting, poaching, and habitat loss have reduced the numbers of many species to the danger point. Only animals that are not threatened may be exported. On occasion, a country will make a gift of one of its rare animals to another country. For example, China gave two giant pandas to the United States in the early 1970s.

About 80 percent of the animals zoos acquire are born in other zoos. Self-sustaining populations of many species exist in zoos and research centers, and any extra animals are made available to other zoos.

A turning point in Willie's life came in 1988. That year Zoo Atlanta opened the Ford African Rain Forest, a brand-new home for Willie and the zoo's other lowland gorillas. It was a large open-air enclosure designed to resemble the rain forest of Willie's native central Africa.

The Way Willie Likes It

Willie's rain forest home is just one example of the far-reaching changes that have taken place in zoos in recent years. Zoos no longer feel their primary mission is simply to collect and display as many different species of animals from around the world as they possibly can. They no longer believe that the more unusual animals a zoo has, the better it is. Instead, zoos are changing into conservation parks that cooperate to help save animals threatened with extinction. The first step toward this goal was to get rid of the cages and change the way zoo animals lived.

When Willie was let out of his cage into his new home, he found himself in a large grassy area leading to a gradually rising, rock-covered slope. All around the edges of the slope were trees and plants similar to those in his African home.

In no time, Willie acted like a different animal. He was no longer bored or easily angered. There were tree branches he could pull to test his strength or bend into a nest for his afternoon siesta, and there was a rocky hillside he could climb. More important, he had company. He shared his new home with three females, and other groups of gorillas lived nearby.

Gorillas and other primates were once housed in small cages like these.

Zoo Atlanta's lowland gorilla exhibit is similar to the animals' natural habitat.

Willie could finally act like the silverback he was. He could have his own family and be the dominant male.

Willie had not lost the instinct for peaceful family life that gorillas live by in the wild. He watched over his family when it was feeding or resting, ever alert for danger. His companions could chase each other and wrestle, knowing he was there to protect them. Every so often, he would cup his hands and thump his chest to show the females and nearby rival males who was boss. Willie B. had finally become a real gorilla. In February 1994, he became a father as well.

Three other gorilla groups share Zoo Atlanta's African Rain Forest enclosure with Willie's family. They are kept apart from each other by trees and small hills that mark their territories, just the way it would be in Africa. The gorillas spend their time looking for bamboo shoots and leaves to eat, grooming each other, napping between meals, or just resting.

Willie's story has a happy ending. But the best part is that he is not alone in his good fortune. Thousands of other zoo animals throughout the world have been moved into new homes that replaced the old, cramped cages in which they lived before.

Lessons from Germany

Housing animals in open-air, natural enclosures is not a new idea. The first to use such a setting was Karl Hagenbeck at the Hamburg Zoo, Germany, in 1907. He moved antelopes into a grassy, open area. To add a touch of drama, he placed a pride of lions just behind them. Visitors to the zoo were startled to find lions living next to antelopes. They could not see the moat that separated the predators from their prey.

Hagenbeck's novel idea of allowing animals to move about freely in large open spaces caught on. He was asked to redesign the Detroit Zoo in the 1930s. His ideas were also used in New York's Bronx Zoo, Chicago's Brookfield Zoo, and the San Diego Zoo.

But large-scale redesigning of zoos didn't begin until the 1960s, when natural habitats of wild animals around the world began to shrink in size, and scores of species dwindled to the point of vanishing. Zoo designers traveled to the animals' natural habitats in faraway places to study not only what the habitats looked like but how the animals used the space and behaved in it. Housing animals in spaces that were as close to the animals' habitats as the designers could make them was an important step in the struggle to save endangered species.

Taking Down the Bars

Zoo designers try to satisfy the physical and social needs of animals, even in small spaces, to give them the illusion of freedom. The happy result is that animals have more to do and are more active. The more natural the environment, the more alert and spirited the animals are.

They no longer appear to be lazy. They do not pace back and forth for hours or stare into space, as they did when they were confined in cages. In their new homes, the wild creatures are free to act like themselves. They can nest, scent their territory to warn competitors to stay away, and hide in remote places to relax. They can mingle with their own social group or with various other species that normally live in the same ecosystem in the wild. Most important, in natural settings many animals that had never before reproduced in captivity are having young.

The animals are encouraged to look for food the way they would in the wild. Chimpanzees in their natural habitat often

Zoo enclosures need not look exactly like wild habitats for animals to feel at home.

poke sticks into termite mounds and scoop the insects clinging to the sticks into their mouths. One zoo has placed special cement mounds in its ape display area. When chimps push sticks into holes in the sides of the mounds and pull them back out, they find them covered with honey. In this way, the chimps learn how to use a tool. The chimps also spend a good part of each day searching in nooks and crannies for bananas and other fruit that zoo personnel have hidden. Finding their own food makes them less dependent on humans, and it makes life more interesting for the chimps.

The new zoo habitats blend real and artificial trees and rocks. There are places where animals can find privacy, but there are also features that bring the animals into view—waterfall-fed pools where tigers can take a dip, heated rocks for pythons to bask on, leafy treats for antelopes to eat, and steep cliffs for mountain goats to climb. Apes can swing through 50-foot-high trees, and there are open spaces where they can groom one another, feed and care for their young, or simply doze in the sun.

Exhibits are planned around climate zones. The Audubon Zoo in New Orleans features a swamp with alligators, otters, and turtles. The Seattle Zoo has a ladder for salmon to leap over to reach their spawning area. Local exhibits of the Amazonian rain forest, the Himalayan highlands, or the desert of the American Southwest are biology classrooms for people of all ages. Next to the real thing, zoos are the best places to enjoy the sounds and the sights of faraway, exotic places and the animals and plants that live in them. In fact, the exhibits are so realistic and the animals behave so naturally that researchers have set up observation posts inside the enclosures to conduct field studies.

The plants in the enclosures are kinds that do well in the areas where the zoos are located. They may not necessarily include the same plants found in the animals' habitats. To simulate the feel of the savanna in a giraffe enclosure, designers may plant honey locusts. These are trees that look like African acacias but can withstand freezing temperatures. Honeysuckle and hawthorn bushes give the impression of wet tropical plants for rain forest landscapes. The animals adjust easily to the differences, and zoogoers experience the animals and plants side by side. Zoo designers are careful to supply enough plants to make animals feel at home, but not so many that the animals are hidden.

Designers also give a lot of attention to special effects that imitate nature. Tropical rainstorms douse forest displays every so often, forcing animals to take cover. The showers are accompanied by tape-recorded thunder and flashes of lightning from strobe lights. Speakers fill the air with bird calls and the shrieks of howler monkeys. Modern zoo exhibits not only mimic natural settings but give the impression that the animals are dangerously close to each other. Species that are enemies in the wild are separated by concealed moats, bamboo-covered fences, and artificial ponds that hide submerged barriers. Carefully placed walkways bring visitors close to the wild animals. Glass walls separate visitors from animals, but the glass is lit in such a way as to remove any reflection. The walls are, in fact, invisible.

Close Encounters

With the sights and sounds of reality all around them, it's easy for zoogoers to believe they're walking in the wide-open spaces of the African savanna and that at any moment a lion may walk by. As they follow a twisting path through lush tropical vegetation, they can imagine that a jaguar is ready to pounce from

The Phoenix Zoo's ibex enclosure has the kind of terrain the animals inhabit in the wild.

one of the trees. Visitors are on the same level as nature and they feel the excitement of dangerous places.

But zoogoers sense something deeper than the feeling of being in the real world of the wild kingdom. As they wander the trails, they see creatures that no longer appear weird or lonely, as they did when they were in cages. They also see beautiful wild places that are similar to the natural homes of the animals. This experience increases visitors' understanding of and respect for the world we live in and the creatures that share it with us. There's no better way to grab zoogoers' attention, help them appreciate how diverse and complicated the environment is, and encourage them to support the preservation of wild animals in their natural habitats.

What visitors don't see is what goes on behind the scenes, in the zoos' laboratories and offices. There the battle is being fought to save endangered species and to educate the public about the plight of wildlife. If the zoos fail in that struggle, they won't have to worry about displays of animals in the future. There simply won't be any animals left to display.

Chapter Three

OPERATION NOAH'S ARK

In the Bible story, God instructed Noah to save the animals of the earth from the Great Flood. So Noah built an ark and placed two of each species, one male and one female, in it. Then he waited 40 days and 40 nights for the floodwaters to ebb so that he and all the living things that were with him could go forth from the ark and multiply and fill the land. This was a big job, but compared to the challenge facing modern zoos, Noah had it easy.

As in the story of Noah, disaster is threatening the world's wildlife. But the peril this time springs from a different source. An ever rising tide of humankind is overrunning the habitats of wild animals, crowding them into smaller and smaller spaces, upsetting the balance of nature, and polluting the environment. This time it's not a single ark that has been summoned to the rescue, but a fleet of modern-day Noah's arks: the zoos.

The wilderness and its creatures began to vanish at an alarmingly rapid rate in the mid-1950s. At that time, zoos and animal reserves were the only places with the knowledge and facilities to try to save animals that were in trouble in the wild.

Giraffes are not endangered, but their available habitat is being reduced by the encroachment of humans.

The zoos already had some experience doing conservation work. It was natural that they would lead the fight against extinction, even as they continued to be places where visitors could see strange and wonderful creatures.

Name changes show the importance some zoos place in their new role. For example, the zoo once called the New York Zoological Park, popularly known as the Bronx Zoo, has been renamed the International Wildlife Conservation Park. The park is carrying out more than 150 conservation programs in 40 different countries. This is just one institution, although one of the largest, in a worldwide network committed to rescuing endangered animals. Most major zoos employ highly trained specialists as part of their full-time staffs, in addition to curators, veterinarians, and animal keepers. These experts include scientists who specialize in animal conservation, nutrition, and breeding, and landscapers who understand the animals' native ecosystems.

Difficult Choices

In the beginning of the zoos' rescue effort, the number of species listed as endangered was small. Within a few decades, the number was immense and growing every day. The International Union for the Conservation of Nature (IUCN) keeps track of endangered species in its Red Data Books. The books contain information on endangered animal and plant species and their habitats. The information is prepared country by country around the world.

Because the number of endangered species is so large, it is impossible to save each and every one of the animals on the list. But many conservationists believe that saving even a small number is better than saving none at all. The mission of the

Types of Breeding

Inbreeding—the mating of animals within the same species that are closely related to one another. Humans inbreed animals to reinforce desirable traits, such as high quality wool in sheep. Inbred animals are more likely than others to have birth defects, high death rates, or low fertility rates, and are often vulnerable to disease. This tendency of inbred animals to have health problems is called inbreeding depression.

Outbreeding—the opposite of inbreeding. It refers to the mating of animals that are not closely related. Humans outbreed animals to try to get rid of health problems caused by inbreeding.

Crossbreeding—the mating of individuals from different subspecies or breeds of the same species. Humans crossbreed animals to combine desirable traits from two different breeds.

zoos is to get as many endangered animals as possible safely aboard the arks. Conservation biologists have to decide which of the thousands of critically endangered species they should attempt to save and which they cannot help.

To help make the selection, the American Zoo and Aquarium Association (AZA) created a committee that works with member zoos to compile a list of endangered species. The list includes those species that are near extinction but for which there is still hope. From this list, they select only species that meet certain requirements. There must already be enough individuals of the species in zoos to maintain a healthy breeding population for some time to come. There must be qualified professionals available to manage the breeding program. The species must have a good chance of breeding successfully in captivity. Then there can eventually be a large enough population for the species to be returned to its natural home. It's considered wise to spread the responsibility for each species among several zoos. If disease in one zoo were to kill all the animals there, members of the species would still be alive elsewhere.

Survival of the Fittest

One requirement in any breeding program is that animals to be mated must not be closely related to each other. Livestock and dog breeders deliberately inbreed animals to get certain traits, such as cows that produce a lot of milk, or dogs with uniform characteristics. But these inbred lines often develop health problems. Most human societies prohibit brother-to-sister and cousin-to-cousin marriages. Long ago, people noticed that the youngsters of such pairings were more likely than others to suffer from various physical disorders. At the beginning of the twentieth century, the new science of genetics provided an explanation for this observation.

All organisms inherit genes from each of their parents. These genes help to determine the organism's appearance, behavior, fitness to survive in a particular environment, and other hereditary characteristics. The collection of genes found in a particular population is called its gene pool. Many different genes are found in each of the earth's organisms, and a wide variety of combinations can result from each mating. The rich variety of plant and animal species on earth is the result of this genetic diversity.

Not all of an individual's traits and behaviors are genetically determined. Young female primates learn how to care for infants by observing other females.

Some alleles, or versions, of genes cause diseases, birth defects, or other problems, such as the inability to produce offspring, or high infant death rates. Some of these "bad" alleles are recessive. That is, their effects do not appear in the offspring unless they are received from both parents.

If two individuals that mate are not closely related, the chances that both parents will have the same harmful alleles are small. But if the parents are closely related, the alleles they carry are more likely to be the same. A good percentage of their young may get a double dose of a "bad" allele and develop a harmful hereditary condition. Individuals in small pop-

How Traits Are Inherited

Genetics is the study of the laws of heredity. These laws govern the transmission of traits, such as eye color, from parent to offspring. Each individual inherits a set of genes from each of its parents. It is these genes that provide the coded instructions of heredity.

Each gene carries instructions that influence one or more traits. An inherited trait may be governed by one gene or by many genes. Within a species there may be several different versions, or alleles, of a particular gene. For example, one allele of the human eye color gene produces brown eyes, and another produces blue eyes.

Some alleles are more powerful than others. The more powerful alleles are called dominant alleles, and the weaker ones are called recessive alleles. If an individual receives a dominant allele for a trait from either or both of its parents, it will possess the dominant version of the trait. In order for the recessive version of the trait to appear, the individual must receive the recessive allele from both parents.

For example, in humans the allele for brown eyes is dominant. People who inherited the allele for brown eyes from either or both of their parents have brown eyes. Only those people who inherited the allele for blue eyes from both parents have blue eyes, because the allele for blue eyes is recessive.

Recessive alleles may carry instructions for harmful characteristics, such as low fertility rates or physical abnormalities. An individual that receives a dominant allele from one parent and a recessive allele from the other is called a carrier. Carriers of a recessive allele show the physical characteristics of the dominant allele but may give the recessive allele to their offspring.

Genes are sometimes permanently changed by exposure to radiation or chemicals. Such a change is called a mutation. If a mutation occurs in an egg or sperm cell, it may be passed on to the offspring. Most mutations cause harmful conditions, but some may help individuals survive and adapt to changes in their environment.

ulations tend to be closely related to one another. As a result, the same genetic problems may affect most of the members of the population.

Conservation biologists feel that when a species is reduced to fewer than 50 individuals it is in immediate danger due to inbreeding among the animals. But even 50 individuals of a species will not insure its survival. It is estimated that 500 individuals gives the average species enough genetic variety for it to survive. Even then, it is not safe to keep all the animals of a species concentrated in one small area. Fire, a hurricane, a viral infection, or some other natural disaster could wipe out an entire population at once.

A species that has a diverse pool of genes is better able to survive disease or changes in climate. If a species has a variety of alleles, there are likely to be at least a few individuals that inherit

There is very little genetic variety among cheetahs. An outbreak of disease could easily wipe out an entire population.

the physical traits they need in order to survive and adapt. These traits will then be passed on from generation to generation. This is how new species evolve.

Computer Dating

Before the 1970s, inbreeding was common in zoos because the number of animals held in captivity was small. Some endangered species were also inbreeding in the wild. Habitat destruction had crowded small groups of animals into isolated areas that were cut off from each other by human habitation, roads, and farmland. The animals had a limited selection of mates available to them, and they could not roam to distant places to find others of their kind.

The Species Survival Plans (SSP) program was set up by the AZA in 1981. Its purpose is to preserve the gene pools of en-

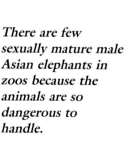

There are few sexually mature male Asian elephants in zoos because the animals are so dangerous to handle.

dangered species and to improve chances that only unrelated animals are mated in zoos. The SSP program concentrates on a limited number of species that can be bred successfully.

An SSP coordinator is chosen for each selected species. The coordinator works with experts in many zoos to design a master plan for matching unrelated animals to assure maximum genetic diversity. The master plan uses information kept in studbooks, which are official records of the ancestry of individual animals. The information is analyzed with the help of computers, and sound breeding recommendations are made.

The Species Survival Plans take into consideration the difficulty and expense involved in transferring an animal between zoos. Animals being moved undergo a great deal of stress, and some die in transit. Also, zoo visitors become attached to particular animals and may object if they are moved to other zoos. Great pains are taken to avoid disrupting animals' social groupings.

An important tool in the management of breeding programs is the International Species Information System (ISIS). This computerized system was established in 1974 by Dr. Ulysses Seal. The system lists information about hundreds of thousands of animals in over 300 zoos in nearly 40 countries. We may think of it as a computer dating service for animals. The information recorded for each animal includes date of birth, place of birth or capture, sex, behavioral patterns, illnesses, reproductive history, who its parents are, where its parents came from, and other important facts.

The ISIS system correlates this information, provides recommendations for SSP coordinators, and makes projections on the outcome of breeding and reintroduction programs. For example, ISIS was consulted about plans to reintroduce the golden lion tamarin, a squirrel-sized monkey, to Brazil. The system predicted that the habitat that had been reserved for the tamarins would not be large enough to support the animals. A different plan was designed, and it has proved to be more successful.

The SSP program and ISIS have opened a new era of cooperation among 164 zoos and aquariums in North America. Institutions that once were competitive loan and exchange their animals to ensure crossbreeding. Europe, Japan, India, and Australia have species survival plans for their zoos, as well.

Bozie, a female Asian elephant at Chicago's Lincoln Park Zoo, is a good example of how ISIS helps zoos' breeding efforts. At 15, Bozie was sexually mature, and the zoo's personnel were eager for her to mate. There was one problem, however. The zoo had no male Asian elephant. A suitable mate would have to be found elsewhere.

The ISIS system came to Bozie's aid. The "dating service" had a perfect mate for her, a male named Onyx at the Dickerson Park Zoo in Springfield, Missouri. Bozie was shipped to Missouri, became pregnant, and was returned to Chicago. In October 1990, 22 months later, she gave birth to a 270-pound calf who was named Shanti. Shanti's birth was good news for the critically endangered Asian elephant. This species does not breed well in zoos, and the wild populations have declined dramatically because of habitat destruction and ivory poaching.

A Formula for Success

Successful breeding programs require much more than computer dating. Conservation biologists must know the social preferences of captive animals. For example, gorillas like to live in large family groups. They are not happy living in pairs and will not reproduce under such an arrangement. On the other

The black rhinoceros prefers to live alone in a large open area. Even a large zoo has space to properly house only a few.

hand, tigers and rhinoceroses are loners, preferring a solitary existence and the opportunity to escape observation. Chimpanzees have close social ties with their families, but will mate only with unrelated partners. Young female primates need to observe and imitate their own mothers or other females in their group in order to learn maternal behavior. Other animals, such as flamingos, gather in large groups to choose mates.

Scientists also must know how habitat affects captive animals' reproductive success. Rhinos prefer to have large spaces around them, while cats and bears do not seem to mind living in confined areas. Hoofed animals, such as deer, bison, and antelope,

Preserving the Genes of Endangered Species

In order for endangered species to survive, their gene pool must be as large as possible. Conservationists realize that they cannot save the entire gene pool of every species, but they hope to preserve at least 90 percent of the genes each species has.

The number of animals needed to retain the genetic diversity of a species depends on many factors. These include the life span of the species, the length of time individuals need to become sexually mature, how often they breed, the number of offspring in each litter, and the ratio of males to females in the population.

The minimum number of animals needed to maintain at least 90 percent of the gene pool of a species is called an ideal population. Conservationists hope to keep an ideal population of each endangered species safe in the world's zoos for the next 200 years.

The number of animals in an ideal population is different for each species. For black-footed ferrets, a minimum of 1,200 individuals is needed to preserve 90 percent of the current genetic diversity. For the Siberian tiger, an ideal population would be at least 140 animals, and for the Arabian oryx, at least 95 animals. Additional animals provide a safeguard against accidents or other unforeseen events.

reproduce easily in zoos. The same is true of tigers, but small cats are less likely to reproduce in captivity.

Biologists must tailor each breeding program to the living and breeding requirements of the particular species. They must provide living arrangements that make animals feel at home and give them a sense of security. They must decide what number of animals are needed in a program. They also must determine how the changes animals have undergone in captivity will affect their reintroduction to the wild. Such changes include the balanced diet provided by zoos, which eliminates the need for animals to hunt for food. Technology is helping scientists make some of these decisions. But most of the problems have to be solved by long and careful observation of each species, both in the field and in zoos.

Some biologists estimate that zoos can rescue and support 200 to 500 endangered species until the animals can be reintroduced into their former habitats. Time and money are important limitations on zoo breeding programs. Species are disappearing at an increasingly rapid pace, and zoos depend to a great extent on contributions from private donors to carry on their work.

Space is equally important for breeding programs. Many zoos simply do not have adequate room to breed additional endangered species. Some zoos are developing new programs to ease the overcrowding. The National Zoo in Washington, D.C., and the International Wildlife Conservation Society of New York have established conservation parks at Front Royal, Virginia, and at St. Catherines Island, Georgia, respectively. Other zoos have or are planning similar reserves devoted exclusively to conservation. Even so, space will continue to be limited.

Too Little, Too Late?

Not everyone agrees on the value of captive breeding programs. Some people feel that what is going on in zoos and research centers is unnatural. Species in the various programs, they say, depend on human intervention for their safety and will be vulnerable when they are returned to the wild. They claim

Most attempts to breed giant pandas in zoos have failed.

that present programs ignore the fact that wild animals live in complicated ecosystems, with each animal depending on others in various ways. In a zoo, animals do not have the relationships they would have had with their neighbors in the wild.

The critics add that the present number of breeding programs is tiny compared to the number of endangered species. They say the public is getting a false sense of success. Some species have been returned to the wild and are doing well, but most attempts to breed species such as the cheetah and the giant panda have failed.

Other people say that captive breeding is too little and comes too late to save many species. They believe the goal of zoos should be to educate the public about the causes of extinction, such as overhunting, poaching, and especially the accelerating destruction of wildlife habitats.

To help meet these objections and promote a closer relationship between people and nature, many zoos are evolving into bioparks. In addition to animal exhibits, these places have botanical gardens, aquariums, natural history museums, and even anthropological museums. Bioparks present a well-rounded picture of the entire spectrum of life on earth and help people understand how ecosystems work. They help give people a sense of respect for wildlife and what the loss of species means to our world.

Hope in Technology

Species are vanishing at an alarming rate because of human encroachment, and we cannot foresee what humanity's need for land will be in 200 years. It makes sense to most scientists to keep some species afloat in the various zoo arks, even if there is little hope that all these species will one day thrive again in the wild.

The number of species that can benefit from SSP programs is far larger than can fit in the arks. But the new Noahs are continuing their work with the sense of urgency a doctor feels when treating a seriously ill patient. The doctor must keep the patient alive until the proper cure is found. Until humanity succeeds in controlling its destructive ways, zoos and animal reserves will remain the only rescue stations for the thousands of species tottering on the brink of extinction.

In the meantime, science has provided some innovative approaches that may help save many thousands more species than we once thought possible. These new techniques increase the effectiveness of the zoos' breeding and conservation programs. Even though these innovations are still in the early stages of development, scientists hope that through their use more of our precious wildlife can be saved for future generations.

American SSP Programs

There are about 60 SSP programs in American zoos. Most are for large animals. The majority are mammals, but birds, reptiles, amphibians, fish, and invertebrates are also included. Large animals are popular in zoos, and they are also the ones zoos have been most successful in breeding.

Visitors to a zoo can identify an animal that is part of an SSP program by a sign displayed near its enclosure. The sign shows the silhouette of a mother rhino and her calf. As of July 1994, SSP programs were in effect for these species:

Addax	Goeldi's monkey
African wild dog	Golden lion tamarin
Andean condor	Gorilla
Arabian oryx	Grevy's zebra
Aruba Island rattlesnake	Haplochromine cichlids
Asian elephant	Hartmann's mountain zebra
Asian lion	Humboldt penguin
Asian rhinoceros	Indian rhinoceros
Asian small-toed otter	Jaguar
Bali mynah	Lion-tailed macaque
Barasingha	Madagascar ground boa
Black lemur	Maned wolf
Black rhinoceros	Mexican gray wolf
Black-footed ferret	Micronesian kingfisher
Chacoan peccary	Mongoose lemur
Cheetah	Okapi
Chimpanzee	Orangutan
Chinese alligator	Orinoco crocodile
Cinereous vulture	Partula snail
Drill	Przewalski's horse
Gaur	Puerto Rican crested toad
Giant panda	Pygmy chimpanzee
Gibbon	Pygmy hippopotamus

An infant lion-tailed macaque snuggles close to its mother.

Radiated tortoise
Red panda
Red wolf
Rodrigues' fruit bat
Ruffed lemur
Scimitar-horned oryx
Siberian tiger

Snow leopard
Spectacled bear
Sumatran rhinoceros
Tree kangaroo
Virgin Islands boa
White rhinoceros
White-naped crane

With help from science, the bongo is returning to Mount Kenya.

Chapter Four

THE FROZEN ZOO

By the early 1980s, the bongo had nearly vanished from the lower slopes of Mount Kenya, Africa's second-highest mountain. The bongo is a beautiful species of antelope found only in East Africa. But beauty has never helped any wild animal survive. In fact, beautiful fur, tasty meat, or bones that are thought to possess magical or medicinal powers have sentenced animals of many species to death. The bongo was disappearing from its few remaining habitats because of overhunting.

In 1984, just when the bongo's future appeared hopeless, a new technique was perfected at the Cincinnati Zoo's Center for Reproduction of Endangered Wildlife (CREW). A fertilized egg was removed from a bongo at the Los Angeles Zoo and transported to the Cincinnati Zoo. The embryo was successfully transferred to an eland, a species of antelope closely related to the bongo and common in some parts of Africa. The surrogate-mother technique has been used on domestic cattle for some time, but this was the first attempt to transfer an embryo from one wild species to another. Some months after the transfer, a healthy baby bongo was born to the eland and took its first unsteady steps.

The Kenyan Wildlife Service and CREW are cooperating to collect embryos from bongos on a preserve in Kenya and in the Cincinnati Zoo and transfer them to elands. The elands will then be released at Mount Kenya, which has been made into a protected national park, to give birth to bongo calves. Eland mothers, it is hoped, will not only care for their bongo off-spring but will also teach them the skills they need to survive in the wild. Parent animals pass on complex behaviors to their off-spring from generation to generation, but scientists have a dif-ficult time teaching these skills to zoo-born animals.

Science Fiction or Fact?

The embryo-transfer procedure requires skill and extensive knowledge of animal physiology. A female animal is given hor-mone injections to cause her ovaries to produce a number of eggs. The eggs are fertilized by artificial insemination, a tech-nique in which sperm is collected from a male and inserted into a female's reproductive tract. The resulting embryos are col-lected before they can attach to the wall of the uterus. They are kept in a solution supplemented with nutrients and antibiotics until they can be implanted in the uterus of a surrogate mother. A number of embryos can be collected at one time from a single female. At this stage, each embryo is no larger than a particle of dust.

Embryos grow by cell division. First the fertilized egg cell di-vides in two, and then each of the new cells divides. The process repeats many times. A very young embryo's cells are still generalized. That is, they have not begun to change to spe-cialized organ, skeleton, or skin cells. If a very young embryo splits in half, each half can become a separate embryo. These embryos are genetically identical. A group of genetically identi-cal organisms is called a clone, and any process that results in a clone is called cloning. Since embryo splitting produces two or more genetically identical embryos, it is a form of cloning.

Embryo splitting can occur naturally, resulting in identical twins. But scientists have learned how to artificially split embryos. They do this to produce more offspring of some rare animals.

Sometimes the collected embryos are used immediately. But if they are to be kept for some time, or if they are to be moved to a distant location, they are frozen. The controlled freezing technique is called cryopreservation. The embryos are sealed in a plastic straw, and they are cooled slowly to below freezing. Then they are placed in a liquid nitrogen bath to bring their temperature to -383 degrees Fahrenheit. The extreme cold causes the embryos' cell functions to stop. The embryos remain alive but dormant until they are thawed for insertion into the uterus of a surrogate mother. Cryopreservation is also used to store sperm and eggs of many species.

Scientists believe there is no limit to the time sperm, eggs, or embryos can remain frozen without suffering damage. Calves of domestic livestock have been produced from sperm that had remained frozen for 50 years. What is important is the technique of freezing and thawing. But to prevent any unhappy surprises, some conservationists recommend that the frozen stock of genetic materials be replaced every 10 years. The old stock can be used to produce offspring. Their sperm and eggs can be frozen, in turn, to begin the cycle all over again.

One advantage in transferring embryos is that a female animal can become fertile again soon after a set of embryos is removed. One female can therefore produce many offspring. Another advantage is that new genes can be introduced into a group without moving any animals. Embryo transfers from bongos to elands are a novel way of reintroducing bongos to an area from which they had been hunted nearly to extinction.

Eventually, this technique could be used to revive many more rare species.

The main difficulty in using the embryo-transfer technique is timing. The estrus cycle must be figured out carefully, because the transfer must be done when the female is capable of producing eggs. Female elephants, for example, are fertile just one day every 16 weeks. And giant pandas are receptive only two days a year. Knowledge of the estrus cycle of domestic animals can be obtained by measuring the rise and fall of hormones in their blood. But it's difficult to take blood samples of wild animals. They have to be tranquilized first, and this procedure stresses them. Another difficulty is that not all sperm cells have the strength to penetrate the membrane of an egg to fertilize it. And the sperm of some species, such as monkeys and cats, is difficult to freeze and thaw without killing it.

In vitro fertilization is another technique that has been useful in propagating wild species. Eggs are taken from a female and placed in a test tube or a shallow dish. Sperm is added to fertilize them. After fertilization, healthy embryos are inserted into the womb of the natural mother or a surrogate. This technique is especially useful when animals have problems conceiving naturally, as when sperm are not strong enough to travel on their own to the female's uterus.

In 1991, Dr. David Wildt of the National Zoo in Washington, D.C., succeeded in producing two healthy Bengal tiger cubs by collecting eggs from a female Bengal and fertilizing them in a vial with sperm from a male Bengal. As soon as the eggs were fertilized and dividing, he implanted them in a female Siberian tiger. Both varieties of tigers are rare, but there are many female Siberian tigers in zoos that can serve as surrogate mothers.

Waiting for Life

Embryo transfer and in vitro fertilization are used extensively at CREW. The center's headquarters and research facility has glass-walled labs so that visitors can see technicians freezing sperm and embryos. Visitors can also watch through a monitor connected to a powerful microscope as researchers use precision tools thinner than a human hair to split feline embryos into identical parts. State-of-the-art exhibits explain the complex research required for successful wildlife conservation. The facilities at the center are the finest in the world. They include laboratories, a surgical room, a greenhouse, cold-storage areas, and a tissue culture incubator in which plant or animal cells are grown to preserve their genes.

Many of the experiments at CREW focus on plant breeding.

Scientists at CREW have used the eland to test many of their breeding techniques.

Cryopreservation, commonly called the Frozen Zoo, forms the heart of the research at CREW. Here scientists are preserving eggs, sperm, embryos, and tissue of over 500 species of endangered animals, as well as tissue and seeds of many rare plants. This storehouse of priceless genetic material will eventually be used to produce more of these rare animals and plants. But first the technology must be perfected, habitats must be made safer, and appropriate surrogate mothers for the rare animal embryos must be identified.

Some remarkable firsts in assisted reproduction have taken place at CREW. The center was first to create a Frozen Zoo to preserve genetic materials of wild animals. In 1983, an eland was born to an eland surrogate mother in the first fresh-embryo transfer in a wild species. The same technique was repeated successfully with an embryo that had remained frozen for over a year. In 1988, an eland was born from one half of a split embryo. The other half remains in CREW's Frozen Zoo.

The center also boasts the world's first successful artificial insemination of a feline species. This was accomplished in 1983 and resulted in the birth of a Persian leopard cub. The procedure was made especially difficult because female cats do not produce and discharge eggs on a regular schedule, as most other mammals do. In 1989, an endangered Indian desert cat was born to a domestic cat through in vitro fertilization at the center. This was the first time a cat had been chosen to act as a surrogate mother for another species.

In 1994, CREW scientists injected the sperm of a domestic cat directly into eggs taken from two female domestic cats. The eggs were incubated in a laboratory culture. One of the resulting embryos was inserted in the uterus of a female cat. After a normal gestation period, a healthy kitten was born. This technique can be used to propagate endangered cat species.

Interspecies embryo transfers between wild and domestic animals have been successfully carried out in other zoos, as well. The gaur is a species of wild cattle of imposing size with a dark brown coat and white stockings. The gaur is rare, both in its natural habitat—in India and the forests of Southeast Asia—and in zoos. In 1987, a gaur calf was born to a common Holstein cow at the International Wildlife Conservation Park in New York.

The London Zoo has successfully bred two Przewalski's horse foals by transferring embryos to pony mares. Przewalski's horses are smaller than domesticated horses. They are grayish yellow in color and are distinguished by a stiff upright black mane. They are extinct in Mongolia and China, their ancestral home, but they are flourishing in zoos. There are plans to reintroduce them to their former habitat if they can be taught how to forage the open range and watch out for enemies.

Genetic Sleuthing

Advances in genetic analysis are also helping zoo biologists preserve and monitor species under their care. Found near the center of each plant or animal cell is a structure called the nucleus. Inside the nucleus are a number of small threadlike objects called chromosomes. The chromosomes are made of several chemical substances, including DNA (deoxyribonucleic acid). The DNA molecule is shaped like a long, twisted rope ladder. The genes containing the coded instructions that govern heredity are pieces of the DNA ladder. Genes are strung together along the DNA molecule like pearls on a necklace.

Each individual's DNA pattern is unique. Like fingerprints, the genetic code can be used to identify an individual. A machine called a cytogenic analyzer is used to separate the DNA into a series of bands. The pattern is visible as a row of black bars, much like the bar codes found on packages in the grocery store. Biologists can compare the genetic code of one animal's DNA with that of another animal. They can establish if the animals are related and, if they are, how closely they are related.

Genetic fingerprinting is especially useful when animals are taken from the wild, for it's difficult in that case to know which individuals are related. Identification makes it easier to avoid inbreeding when pairing animals for mating. By looking at DNA patterns, biologists can identify family groups. Since groups living in a specific locality show similarities in their DNA patterns, it is possible to pinpoint the area from which a wild animal came. Biologists can also detect the crossing of closely related species.

Chromosome analysis helps scientists determine the sex of birds that are to be included in breeding programs. It is often difficult to determine the sex of birds because the males and females of many species look exactly alike. Chromosome analysis is also used to determine an animal's species or subspecies.

This technology has been used to examine how whooping cranes are related to one another, and in breeding captive California condors. It has also been used to track down poachers of elephants in Africa. All African elephants may look alike to us, but there are many subtypes that do not mix well in the wild and have evolved differently. Genetic fingerprinting shows the differences among these groups. Scientists analyze the DNA in confiscated elephant tusks and compare it with DNA collected from elephants in various parts of Africa. The scientists can pinpoint the habitat of the elephants the poachers killed, as well as

The Robo Egg

New electronic devices are helping scientists gain knowledge about breeding requirements. This is especially important when working with birds, many of which are difficult to breed in captivity.

The robotic egg, dubbed the robo egg, is shaped like a real egg. It is placed with the other eggs in a bird's nest. The parent birds mistake it for one of their own eggs and incubate it along with the others. Sensing devices inside the robo egg measure temperature and humidity, and how frequently the birds rotate the eggs.

Each species of bird incubates its eggs under specific conditions that are different from those for any other species, so it is critically important to have exact data. The robo egg is helping biologists set up favorable conditions for hatching real eggs of the white-naped crane, a highly endangered species.

the family group to which each elephant belonged. This information shows officials where to start looking for the poachers who sold the confiscated tusks.

Playing God?

Assisted reproduction technology holds great promise for keeping many endangered species from becoming extinct in the twenty-first century and beyond. The potential is great, but research takes years and there are many failures on the road to success. It took three years, for instance, to develop the technique to transfer embryos between members of the same species.

The work being done is rough compared to what conservationists will be able to do in the future. Eventually lasers may allow them to implant embryos with greater precision. The manipulation of genes to change characteristics of an organism also holds promise.

Some scientists feel that the populations of many endangered species are so small that if we don't use all the tools at our disposal those species will vanish forever. Extinction closes out any possibility that a species can adapt itself to changing conditions. If a species can't adapt, it can't survive or develop into a new species. When we save genetic material, however, we're saving the information in the DNA. The biodiversity held in the Frozen Zoo opens new options for the future.

One day, we may be able to create organisms of our own design by rearranging the codes in genes. Scientists know how genes operate. They can manipulate some genes to produce certain characteristics and keep other harmful ones inactive, or eliminate them completely. This is called genetic engineering. Some people feel that it is wrong to manipulate the genes of living creatures. Others fear that genetic engineering may result in the accidental production of dangerous organisms. But the use of these techniques may become common in the future. Until then, the goal is to preserve the creatures we have.

Cloning may offer new possibilities for propagation. In addition to the splitting of embryos, techniques have been developed to grow offspring from the cells of adult animals. The individuals produced in this way grow up to be genetically identical duplicates of the original animal. An advantage of this technique is that scientists can produce great numbers of duplicates. The procedure is controversial, however. Many people are concerned that the research may lead to the cloning of humans. Also, there is no genetic diversity in a group of identical animals.

To people who object to the genetic manipulation involved in cloning, CREW's director, Dr. Betsy Dresser, says that the worst catastrophe is to lose a species. If the world were down to the last five rhinos, she would clone them rather than let them become extinct. Dresser believes the genetics problem can be sorted out later. For example, the Arabian oryx population was once down to very low numbers. The population was increased by inbreeding the few remaining animals, then outbreeding them as the population became more stable. They have been doing well since their reintroduction to the wild.

Reaching Out

Scientists at CREW and the other zoos involved in assisted reproduction are reaching out to other countries. The CREW International program has been organized to share technology developed in Cincinnati with conservationists around the world. Staff members travel to other countries to demonstrate new techniques they have developed that can be applied to na-

A Love for Wildlife

The director of research at CREW is Dr. Betsy Dresser, a Ph.D. in reproductive animal physiology and a professor at the University of Cincinnati Medical Center. She feels it's a pity that the people and technology to freeze dinosaur embryos indefinitely didn't exist 65 million years ago, to keep *Tyrannosaurus rex* and the other giant reptiles from becoming extinct. She fears that one of these days there may be no elephants left, and thinks it would be a tragedy if our grandchildren could see these magnificent animals only in books.

Dresser's love for wildlife began in her early childhood. She read all the books on animals she could find, and she spent her spare time at the Cincinnati Zoo. After high school, she took a job with a firm doing animal research, and she was a volunteer tour guide at the zoo. She went to college on a scholarship, majoring in zoology. She got her doctorate at Ohio State University, and took a job with the zoo upon graduation.

Dresser's first trip to Africa was an important experience for her. She was awed by the sight of wild animals in their own environment. From this experience and her studies in genetics grew her conviction that the best way to save endangered animals is to collect and preserve genetic material. This material is easily transported and can be implanted in animals living in natural habitats.

Dr. Betsy Dresser holds two cats that grew from frozen embryos implanted in a surrogate mother's uterus.

tive animals, and they exchange genetic materials with their hosts. They also invite interns from overseas to spend some time at CREW observing and learning.

Cincinnati's CREW, the San Diego Zoo, the National Zoo in Washington, D.C., and the International Wildlife Preservation Society in New York are freezing and storing genetic material of hundreds of endangered species as insurance against future losses. The genetic information in these DNA samples can be saved for a time when habitats are more secure. Eventually, scientists will have the option to reverse extinction. They will be able to raise from the dead species that have been lost through bad management, habitat destruction, or natural disasters.

It seems fitting that so much of the high-tech work is being done at the Cincinnati Zoo, for this is the place where Martha, the last passenger pigeon, died in 1914. This species of bird was so common in North America in the 1870s that flocks of millions darkened the sky when they flew overhead. In the following few decades, passenger pigeons were slaughtered by hunters. All that remains of the passenger pigeon is its statue on the roof of a small museum at the zoo. But for many other species facing the same dangers, the future doesn't look quite so dismal.

The Parc National des Volcans, in Rwanda, is one of the last remaining refuges of the mountain gorilla.

Chapter Five

A PLANET IN CRISIS

The trek up the dew-drenched slope of the volcano was steep and difficult, but the rewards awaiting us at the end of the trail made the effort worthwhile. We were a small group of eco-tourists, visitors from industrialized countries eager to see wildlife and wild places. We were making the grueling hike in the highlands of the central African country of Rwanda, hoping to see something special. I was eagerly following close behind our machete-swinging guide as he hacked at the thick bamboo forest to open a narrow path. I noticed he kept an eye out for signs of the mountain gorilla family he knew was somewhere nearby.

The first sight of the family took our breath away. They were led by a huge silverback with broad shoulders who showed he was the boss by hooting and thumping his chest. It was a spell-binding moment, and I felt the mystery and raw power of nature. We huddled close to the wet ground and watched quietly for a long time. The family went through its daily activities of eating bamboo leaves, grooming themselves, and napping. The youngsters spent a good deal of time playing.

Despite their fierce reputation, gorillas are peaceful vegetarians that will attack only if they are threatened. Our group was in no danger, we knew, since this family had been habituated to people. Park rangers habituate the gorillas by approaching them slowly, over a series of visits. They go closer to the gorillas on each visit and spend time with them until the gorillas feel comfortable in the presence of humans. On the day of our visit, in fact, two gorilla youngsters overcome by curiosity ambled right up to us to inspect us more closely. It made our day.

On the way down the mountain, we passed through the camp of researcher Dian Fossey, who devoted her life to saving mountain gorillas. As we got closer to the valley, we noticed something that made us uneasy. Acre after acre of bamboo forest on the lower slopes of the volcano had been burned. The land had been turned into pasture for grazing cattle and into farms to grow food. People were settling farther and farther up the mountain, taking the land of the gorillas for their own use. As a result, the gorillas were being squeezed into a shrinking area in the higher altitudes.

Mountain gorillas live in a limited area on the slopes of a few volcanoes in Rwanda and on some isolated mountains in Uganda and Zaire. Because the human population of these countries is soaring, people are invading the gorillas' habitat and competing with them for living space and food. This is the main reason the number of gorillas has declined so dramatically. In 1995, there were only about 300 mountain gorillas alive in Rwanda. There were perhaps an equal number living in neighboring countries.

Human interference has taken other forms, too. Some gorillas are killed when they accidentally get caught in hunters' traps. Others are deliberately shot for trophies. In the past, poachers sometimes killed a whole family of gorillas so that they could capture a baby gorilla to sell to a zoo.

There are laws to protect the gorillas. But there are never enough rangers to enforce the laws. So the battle goes on

Friend of the Mountain Gorilla

Dian Fossey spent 20 years of her life studying the mountain gorillas of central Africa. Famed anthropologist Dr. Louis Leakey sent her to the Virunga Mountains to learn as much as she could about these magnificent animals.

Fossey spent all her time following the gorilla groups, observing and recording their behavior. She won their trust by imitating their behavior, and they came to treat her as a member of their clan. Her work with our closest primate relative has helped us learn about ourselves and how early humans may have lived.

Fossey faced many hardships while working in Africa. Native poachers and local authorities resented her, and living conditions were harsh. But she never, even at the worst of times, considered leaving what had become "her" family of gorillas. The conservation of the mountain gorilla and its habitat became her crusade.

Fossey was killed under mysterious circumstances in 1985. She may have been murdered by poachers who resented her protection of the gorillas. She is remembered as a bold conservationist who dedicated her life to the preservation of the mountain gorilla.

A monument to Dian Fossey stands in the mountain gorilla graveyard at the Karisoke Research Center in Rwanda.

between those who want to protect the gorillas and the farmers, hunters, and poachers who threaten the gorillas' continued existence.

At the beginning of 1995, a civil war took place in Rwanda. Hundreds of thousands of people were killed. There were fears that the gorillas might also have died in this conflict. At the end of the war, however, visitors to Rwanda reported the gorillas had survived, and the new government of Rwanda is committed to protecting them. The challenge of saving the gorillas from extinction will continue.

Upsetting the Balance

Like the gorillas, many other animals and plants are in trouble in the wild because one species, humans, is growing ever more numerous. The World Bank is an agency of the United Nations that helps countries develop their economies by giving them loans and funding big projects. It predicts that the world's 1994 population (about 5.6 billion) will rise to 8.5 billion people by the year 2030 and 10 billion by 2050, unless some form of control is imposed. The population is growing by 95 million people every year, or nearly the 1994 population of Japan.

The fastest growing human populations are in poor, economically underdeveloped countries in Africa, Asia, and South America. The effect on wildlife is devastating. So many more people need so much more land to feed and house themselves. That means that more forests are being cleared, more wetlands filled, and more prairies plowed under, without regard to the wild creatures that live in these areas. Their habitats destroyed, their food supply gone, species of animals that have lived there are vanishing. As Pakistan's prime minister, Benazir Bhutto, warned at the 1994 United Nations Conference on Population

Large tracts of forested land in economically underdeveloped countries have been burned to make room for farms.

and Development, our planet is out of control and moving toward a catastrophe.

If habitat destruction continues at its present pace, it is estimated one quarter of all the world's species of animals in existence in 1995 will vanish by the year 2030. In the 1990s, the rate of extinction reached several species per hour, according to some ecologists. This is a rough guess because no one knows precisely how many species of animals there are. About 1.5 million have been identified, but there are probably at least 10 million. Some scientists believe there may be three times that number.

Extinction is a natural process, and some people say it isn't anything we should worry about. The theory of evolution predicts that just as new species come into existence by adapting to

The Northwest's spotted owl was listed as a threatened species in 1990. The decline of the owl population showed that the entire ecosystem was at risk.

changing conditions, others fail to adapt and become extinct. Much has been made of the extinction of the dinosaurs, which was possibly caused by a change in the earth's climate.

But we have reason to be concerned about the speed at which animals are vanishing. In the past, species usually declined over a long period of time. There was sufficient time for some members of the species to adapt to changing conditions, evolve into a new species, and survive. In modern times, destruction is swift. When extinction happens rapidly, species have no chance to evolve. Humanity's domination of almost every ecosystem is causing whole groups of plants and animals to disappear unnaturally fast.

The species in an ecosystem are interconnected. They depend on each other for their survival. If there are only a few species in an ecosystem, the disappearance of even one species can result in the extinction of several others. If a wide variety of species lives in an ecosystem, each species has many others to depend on. The greater the variety of life present in an ecosystem, the healthier it is. But many species are becoming extinct, and the wonderful diversity of life on which humans and other species depend is collapsing.

Humans are learning that the diversity of life is a direct sign of the condition of the environment. Certain animals, such as the spotted owl in the forests of the northwestern United States, are known as indicator species because their presence indicates that the ecosystem in which they live is healthy. These animals depend on many other species for their survival, so if an indicator species is threatened, it shows that the whole ecosystem is in danger. Every organism plays its part in the balance of nature. While it may be that some species can be lost without causing a catastrophe, no one knows where the limit lies.

In addition to habitat destruction, there are other less direct, but equally dangerous, forms of human interference. People displace some species, either intentionally or unintentionally, by introducing animals from other areas into a habitat. This is especially true when foreign species are brought to island ecosystems that are small and isolated. For example, the venomous brown tree snake was accidentally brought to the Pacific island of Guam in World War II. It swept the island clean of eight unique species of birds, including the Melanesian kingfisher and the Guam rail, by eating their eggs. These birds had previously had no predators. By 1995, only 60 Melanesian kingfishers were left, and all were in zoos.

Humankind all but exterminated the Arabian oryx and the black rhinoceros by overhunting. The Tasmanian wolf, a carnivorous marsupial unique to the island of Tasmania, which is south of Australia, was hunted to extinction in the wild in 1930. The last of this species died in a Tasmanian zoo in 1936. We can add the great auk, the dodo, the passenger pigeon, and many others to the list of species that are now extinct.

Many plants are also in danger of extinction. Some are disappearing because their habitats are limited or because plant-eating animals, such as goats or deer, are overcrowded and have eaten all of the area's vegetation. Other plants are vanishing because humans have introduced foreign plant species that compete aggressively for space with the natives. And there are examples of humans poaching plants, such as the dwarf cactus of the southwestern United States, because they are rare and can be sold for a profit.

Human beings have been the biggest contributors to environmental damage, mostly as an unintended result of our technologies. For example, tanker accidents have spilled millions of gallons of oil, polluting the oceans and killing birds and fishes.

Another example of environmental damage is the effect of DDT (dichloro-diphenyl-trichloroethane), a chemical widely used in the United States in the 1960s to kill pests on crops. Plant-eating animals ingested DDT with their food. Rain also washed DDT off the land into lakes and rivers that carried it to the sea. Peregrine falcons and pelicans ate birds and fish that contained the pesticide. The DDT caused the shells of falcon and pelican eggs to be so thin that they cracked easily. As a result, few chicks hatched, and the birds' populations declined. When DDT was banned by the federal government in 1972, the falcon and pelican populations began to recover.

The earth's atmosphere has also been affected by human technology. The greenhouse effect is a natural process by which

The peregrine falcon is recovering, but the DDT threat remains. Developing countries such as Mexico and Brazil still use the pesticide, mostly to control malaria.

gases such as carbon dioxide help to prevent the earth's heat from escaping into space. Extra carbon dioxide is released when we burn gasoline and when forest fires occur, and our technology also produces other gases that contribute to the greenhouse effect. Rising levels of these "greenhouse gases" may raise the temperature of the earth and bring about the destruction of countless species.

Laws passed by local and national governments play an important part in saving threatened species. At one time, overhunting of whales had reduced their numbers so dramatically that they were headed for extinction. Strict laws against whaling were passed by most of the maritime countries involved in whale hunting. These laws have led to increases in the numbers of many species of whales. For example, in 1994 the California gray whale was the first marine mammal to be removed from the endangered species list. Its population increased from 3,000 in 1973 to 24,000 in 1995. But getting nations to cooperate in protecting endangered species is often difficult. Japan and Norway have resisted the whaling ban because their people traditionally eat whale meat.

The Endangered Species Act of 1973

The Endangered Species Act is a law that was passed by Congress in 1973. It forbids people from hunting, collecting, trapping, importing, exporting, or in any other way harming any species of animal or plant whose continued existence is threatened. Primary responsibility for the enforcement of the act rests with the U.S. Fish and Wildlife Service.

The act protects all species classified as threatened or endangered, whether they have commercial value or not. The protection extends to the preservation of the species' habitats. Assistance is provided to states and even foreign governments to assure this protection.

There are some exceptions to the protection provided by the Endangered Species Act. Natives of Alaska can hunt endangered animals for use as food or shelter. An endangered animal can also be killed if it threatens the life of a human or if it is too sick to survive.

The bald eagle, the national bird of the United States, has made a spectacular comeback thanks to another law, the Endangered Species Act of 1973. In 1978, when this majestic bird was officially added to the endangered list, the number of breeding pairs had declined to fewer than 400. Human population growth was destroying the eagle's habitat, and pollution and hunting were taking their toll. The law made it illegal to hunt eagles and, more importantly, it prohibited developers and forest companies from disturbing eagle habitat. After 20 years of protection, there were over 4,000 breeding pairs of bald eagles in the United States. The comeback of the eagle has become a symbol of the success of the Endangered Species Act.

Nature's Movers and Shakers

Most conservationists and wildlife research biologists agree that the best approach to rescuing an endangered animal is to try to save its habitat or restore its home to its natural condition. They believe that priority should not be placed on saving single species in the artificial environment of zoos, much as that is needed for some species. Their biggest objection is that while zoos work to save one kind of animal, all the others living in the same habitat are left to fend for themselves.

Large mammals like elephants, gorillas, rhinos, and tigers are the most endangered in the wild. They need huge areas in which to live, and they are the most valuable to hunters. As a

Environmental legislation has been successful in keeping many species, including the bald eagle, from becoming extinct.

consequence, they have been under tremendous pressure from humans. These animals also have another problem. Their reproduction is slow. Large mammals reach sexual maturity later than most species, and they have long gestation periods—nearly two years in the case of elephants. Many give birth to just one offspring at a time.

Large mammals are called keystone species, after the wedge-shaped keystone at the top of a building's arch that keeps the arch from collapsing. These species help to keep their ecosystems from breaking down. Preservation of keystone species and their habitats is crucial to the survival of a host of other species that share the same habitat. For example, elephants shape the landscape by knocking down trees and digging water holes when drought occurs. The savanna they create helps grass eaters like antelopes, zebras, and wildebeests to survive. These animals, in turn, fall prey to meat-eating lions, leopards, and hyenas. When keystone species are protected in their habitat, all other species in the habitat benefit.

When keystone species disappear, many other animals vanish with them. These species may not be as well known, but they are important to the earth's biodiversity. If keystone species can be saved in their habitats, a diverse group of other animals that live in the same habitats can also be saved. The populations of many species of large animals, however, are declining at such a rapid rate that zoos remain their best refuge. Their best chance for survival is captive breeding, at least until their habitats can be made safe.

Managing Nature

Loss of habitat is a difficult problem to deal with. Any plan to protect the habitat of an endangered animal must also take the

Sap can be collected from rubber trees without destroying the trees or the rest of the ecosystem.

local people into account. It is important to make certain that they will be able to earn a decent living by some means other than farming or poaching.

Conservationists have to be very creative. Economic pressure is usually on the side of land developers. Those who want to preserve wilderness areas must show that their plans will be financially more rewarding in the long run than developing the land would be. However, people are beginning to realize that the remaining untouched forests, mountains, deserts, and wetlands are more valuable in their natural state than if they were destroyed.

Scientists in the Amazonian rain forest have shown that products harvested without destroying the forest are worth more on a long-term basis than the money to be made by cutting down trees for timber and then raising cattle on the resulting pastureland. They have proposed that areas of rain forest be left as "extractive reserves" under the control of the local inhabitants. These people understand best what riches the jungle can provide, such as nuts, fruits, medicinal plants, and rubber tapped from rubber trees. They are also the ones whose lives are most directly affected by the destruction of the forest. In preserving the forest, the habitat of all the creatures that live there is also preserved.

Ecotourism also holds great promise in helping wildlife and humans coexist. Tourists are encouraged to visit ecologically sensitive areas that are home to rare or threatened species. This helps to educate the tourists about the areas they are visiting, the animals that inhabit them, and what must be done to save the ecosystem.

Tourists in critical natural areas must take great care to avoid damaging the ecosystem or disturbing the wildlife. For example, visitors to the mountain gorillas are taught how to behave so as not to frighten the gorillas and disrupt their peaceful family life. Thoughtful ecotourism always uses the most environmentally sound technology, such as paddled canoes instead of motorboats. Trips are often led by local guides who really know the environment, and polluting and littering are strictly forbidden.

The money that is spent by the visitors can be used to help preserve these areas. The tourist industry employs large numbers of local people. They, in turn, become protectors of wildlife, since their livelihood depends on a healthy ecosystem. Rwanda's Parc National des Volcans is one of the few remaining areas where mountain gorillas survive in East Africa. The

Cheetahs are timid and easily driven away from their prey. Tour guides must be careful not to frighten them.

fees that ecotourists pay to visit the park's gorilla preserve provide much of the money used to pay rangers' salaries and to cover other operating costs.

Ecotourism has grown to become one of the largest industries in such African countries as Kenya and Tanzania. Hundreds of thousands of visitors from all over the world come to see elephants, giraffes, lions, and other large animals roaming free. Tourists who love nature are also visiting the rain forests of Brazil, Peru, and Costa Rica in increasing numbers. The money they spend boosts the local economies and helps maintain the wilderness areas in their natural state.

Another innovative idea is the "debt-for-nature swap." This type of arrangement encourages poor countries with threatened habitats to preserve these lands in exchange for a reduction of the debts they owe richer countries. In the long run, everyone profits from such deals. Habitats are preserved, and pressure is removed from poor countries that feel they must develop their lands in order to make enough money to survive.

Since the World Wildlife Fund pioneered debt-for-nature swaps in 1987, more than $90 million in funds for conservation have been generated. One example is the South American country of Colombia, whose vast Amazonian jungle contains about 10 percent of all plant and animal species. The Colombian government signed an agreement with the U.S. government to reduce the loans they owed the U.S. by $30 million. In exchange, Colombia agreed to protect areas of intact rain forest and to create Ecofundo, an organization that will fund and manage environmental projects in Colombia.

New ideas for accommodating the needs of both animals and people continue to emerge. In the 1940s, about 60 million geese, swans, and other waterfowl spent their winters in the wetlands around the Sacramento River delta just north of San Francisco, California. By the early 1990s, their numbers had sunk to fewer than three million because water had been diverted from the wetlands for human uses such as the cultivation

Teaching People to Save Wildlife

The Jersey Wildlife Preservation Trust was established in 1963 by British author and naturalist Gerald Durrell. It is located on the small island of Jersey in the English Channel. The trust does much of its captive breeding and conservation work in the endangered species' home countries, with help from the governments of those countries. The trust sends its own staff overseas to provide advice and set up breeding colonies, mostly in local zoos that have been renovated to meet modern standards.

Most of the species facing extinction live in developing countries that lack trained personnel to handle recovery programs. To meet this need, the trust has organized an international training center that is housed next to its zoo in Jersey. There, students from various countries learn how to care for species native to their own lands and how to manage conservation and ecology projects. The center offers its graduates a certificate in endangered species management. It is the only institution in the world to do so. The center has trained hundreds of students from more than 60 countries. These training programs are key to the trust's success in aiding endangered species in various areas of the world.

One of the trust's continuing projects is the rescue of the aye-aye. This species is unique to the forests of the island of Madagascar, off the east coast of Africa. The aye-aye is one of the strangest-looking pri-

of rice. Then a partnership of rice growers and environmentalists began working on a plan to bring the birds back without
destroying the farmers' livelihood.

Rice fields are flooded during the rice growing season from

mates on earth. It has enormous eyes, large ears and teeth, and long,
slender fingers ideal for exploring the tiniest crevices. These features
give it a strange, gremlinlike appearance.

The aye-aye is a slow-moving, nocturnal animal, and many of the people of Madagascar think it possesses magical powers. These people believe anyone who encounters an aye-aye in the dark will meet with an
accident or even death. To avoid such meetings, people tend to stay
home at night. This lack of contact between aye-ayes and humans helped
the aye-aye stay out of trouble until the middle of the twentieth century.

People began to cut down Madagascar's great forests in the late 1960s to
make room for coconut and sugar plantations. The aye-aye was left without a home and without food. The only way it could survive was by raid-
ing coconut and sugar farms. The people were faced with a dilemma. They
had to let the aye-aye continue ruining their crops, or they had to give up
their superstitions about the aye-aye's powers. The aye-aye lost. Thousands were slaughtered, bringing the animal to the brink of extinction.

The aye-aye clings to life on a small protected island off the coast of
Madagascar. The Jersey Trust is leading the mission to save this exotic
creature through a breeding program carried out with the help of the
country's government. This effort is matched by an intensive educational
campaign aimed at changing people's attitudes toward this unique part of
their natural inheritance.

The Canada goose is one of many birds that depend on wetlands for their survival.

April to October. When the rice is harvested, the fields are drained to prepare them for next season's planting. Under the new plan, the fields are flooded again during the winter, providing a home not only for waterfowl but for many species of shorebirds as well. The birds' habitat is preserved and the land remains productive.

Ultimately, the wise management of the environment depends on stabilizing the human population and, if possible, reducing its numbers. Henry Kendall, M.I.T. physicist and Nobel Laureate, warns that if we don't control the population ourselves, nature will do it for us through disease and other disasters. Other scientists echo his remarks. They suggest that deadly new epidemics such as AIDS may be nature's reaction to human overpopulation and the resulting upset of the balance of nature.

While some environmentalists concentrate their efforts on preserving areas of the world that are rich in plant and animal life, others are working to preserve individual species that have come to the brink of extinction. A number of captive breeding programs have met with success and may serve as models for future projects.

Chapter Six

THE RETURN OF THE NATIVES

The goal of captive breeding programs isn't to produce animals for life in zoos. It is to increase the animals' numbers enough that they can be taken to an appropriate habitat and form the core group for a flourishing wild population.

Reintroducing animals to their native habitat is a complicated process. It depends not only on breeding sufficient numbers of healthy individual animals but also on finding and protecting a suitable habitat. In addition, zoo-born animals must be taught the skills they need to survive and prosper in the wild.

When these conditions have been met for a particular species, then a plan is developed to release a group to the wild. Such reintroduction schemes are happening in a number of different places around the world, and some of them have been encouragingly successful.

The Arabian Oryx

The Arabian oryx is a beautiful antelope with a white body and chocolate brown markings. It is native to the Arabian Peninsula, one of the driest places in the world, where rain sometimes doesn't fall for years. Like the camel, the oryx has adapted well to its environment and can go for months without drinking water.

The Arabs had been hunting the oryx for food for centuries,

but with the introduction of modern automatic guns and four-wheel-drive vehicles, whole populations were decimated. The last known wild oryxes were shot in 1972. Luckily, there were about a dozen captive animals left in zoos and a few private collections so that an attempt could be made to save the species.

Nine oryxes were shipped from private preserves to the Phoenix and San Diego zoos in the mid-1960s. These zoos were chosen because the climate of the American Southwest is similar to that of Arabia. As the animals began to breed, their offspring were sent to various other zoos. The breeding program was so successful that in 1978 four pairs of oryxes from the San Diego Wild Animal Park were shipped to the Shaumari Reserve in Jordan. In the 1980s, herds were also released in reserves in Saudi Arabia and Oman. By the early 1990s, there were about 100 oryxes living in the wild.

The return of the oryx to Oman, a small country in the Arabian Peninsula, illustrates several important features necessary to any successful reintroduction scheme. First, the animals' new home must be carefully chosen, not only for appropriate habitat but also to ensure the safety of the animals. The Yalooni Plateau in Oman had the perfect climate and vegetation and was remote from human population centers. In addition, the project had the strong backing of the Sultan of Oman, a leader who has taken an active interest in the protection of his nation's wildlife heritage.

The cooperation of the local inhabitants was also crucial to the project's success. The Harassis tribespeople who live on the plateau were interested in participating in the program. The oryx is an important part of their heritage, and they vowed to help protect it. Many local people were trained as wildlife guards and rangers and are employed by the project. So far, not

A number of zoos and wildlife refuges, including this one in Fossil Rim, Texas, maintain breeding populations of Arabian oryxes.

a single oryx has been poached.

In addition to those in Jordan, Saudi Arabia, and Oman, there are thriving oryx herds in Qatar, Abu Dhabi, Bahrain, Dubai, and Israel. The story of the oryx is a positive example of what can be achieved. Unless the breeding program and protection from poachers continue for some time to come, however, the oryx could become endangered once again.

The Golden Lion Tamarin

The case of the golden lion tamarin shows the key role that habitat preservation and renewal play in the reintroduction of an endangered species to its native land. Most people know of the vast tropical rain forests of Brazil's Amazon River Basin. But few know that when the Portuguese first arrived in South America, the Atlantic coastline was also covered with forests that were home to plants and animals found nowhere else. As Brazil was colonized and developed, these forests were cleared. By 1995, just two percent of the area remained forested.

One of the rare creatures that lives in these coastal forests is the golden lion tamarin. A tiny New World monkey, the golden lion tamarin has silky golden fur and a lionlike mane that frames its tiny, inquisitive face. Because of deforestation and because for many years they were captured to be sold as pets and as labora-

Golden lion tamarins were once in great demand as pets.

tory animals, only about 400 lion tamarins remained in the wild by 1966. The crisis point for this species had been reached.

The Bronx Zoo took the lead in saving the lion tamarin. Their first action was to ban the sale of these monkeys by listing them as officially endangered in the IUCN's Red Data Book. In the meantime, two Brazilian biologists started a campaign to convince their government to save part of the lion tamarin habitat and preserve the remaining coastal forest. In 1974, a 12,000-acre tract of land was set aside as a preserve. It was named Poço das Antas, which is Portuguese for "the pool of the tapirs." This site was chosen because it was one of the largest surviving coastal rain forest parcels.

While the fight to preserve a native habitat for the tamarins was going on in Brazil, Dr. Devra Kleiman and other biologists at the National Zoo in Washington, D.C., were developing a captive breeding program to supply tamarins for eventual release in Brazil. A studbook was created to keep track of the different genetic lines so inbreeding could be minimized.

At the beginning of the breeding program, the tamarins' birth and survival rates were poor. But studies of the tamarins' eating habits and reproductive behavior helped the program succeed. It was discovered, for example, that tamarins need sunlight to stay healthy and that they must vary their vegetarian diet with an occasional mouse, lizard, or insect in order to get enough protein to survive and reproduce.

Researchers under Kleiman observed the social life of the tamarins. They found that tamarins are monogamous. Each pair stakes out its own territory, which must be out of sight of other tamarins. Youngsters stay with their parents until another litter is born. As more was learned about the tamarins' eating habits, social life, and ideal mating conditions, management of their housing, diet, and medical care improved and their numbers began to increase. By 1975, there were 72 tamarins in North American zoos. By 1981, there were 261 tamarins, and in 1983, almost 500.

Finally it was decided there were enough animals to risk releasing them in the wild. But the scientists were nervous about returning the zoo-bred tamarins to the jungle. Would they have the survival skills needed to avoid predators and find food?

Kleiman took some of the captive-bred tamarins to Brazil. Before they were released, however, they were taught how to gather their own food in the forest. Biologists showed the tamarins where to look for fruit, how to open fruit for eating, and how to hunt small animals.

In 1984, to the great excitement of all involved, the first golden lion tamarin climbed out of its cage. It looked cautiously around, and, with a great leap, vanished into the Brazilian forest. As of early 1993, 144 tamarins had been released and tracked with radio transmitters. At first the death rate was fairly high. Some were killed by dogs or snakes or unknown illnesses. Others just disappeared. Of the total, 82 have managed to survive the difficult transition period, and 67 offspring have been born to reintroduced tamarins.

Dr. James Dietz and his wife, Lou Anne, have been working in Brazil to ensure that the project continues to succeed. Young Brazilians are being trained to manage the animals, and an innovative habitat restoration project is underway in which native trees are planted in areas that have been deforested. This will increase the available habitat for the tamarins.

Another aspect of the golden lion tamarin project that makes it a model for future projects is the efforts of Lou Anne Dietz. She has worked tirelessly to make local people who live in the

Poço das Antas area aware of the plight of the tamarins. She has enlisted their help to protect newly released animals through lectures, TV and radio programs, posters, and even bumper stickers. As Senegalese conservationist Baba Dioum has observed, ultimately human beings will conserve only what they love, they will love only what they understand, and they will understand only what they are taught.

The Florida Panther

Conservationists are deeply concerned about the success of ongoing efforts to save the Florida panther. Difficult problems with inbreeding and loss of habitat must be overcome for these efforts to succeed.

The Florida panther is not a panther but a large cat that belongs to the same family as the domestic cat. It is a subspecies of the cougar. Cougars are known by various other names, such as catamount, mountain lion, and puma, in different parts of

Biologists have released female cougars in Florida panther habitats in the hope that the cougars will mate with male panthers and produce litters of healthy kittens.

the Americas. The Florida panther is brownish yellow with white markings around its mouth, and its kittens are covered with dark spots. The panther is a powerful predator that feeds on deer and wild hogs.

The Florida panther once thrived across the southeastern section of the United States. In 1995, only 30 to 50 individuals remained in the wild. Ten kittens were caught in 1991 to establish a captive breeding population, but intensive attempts to breed the panther have not proved successful. Their numbers are so low that inbreeding is causing serious genetic problems. Many of the panthers are sterile, and kittens are often born with heart defects. If this situation continues, the Florida panther may be extinct by 2020.

Since the Florida panther cannot recover on its own because of the problems caused by inbreeding, 10 cougars were brought from Texas in 1993 to enlarge the gene pool. It is hoped that this new pool of healthy genes will invigorate the breeding program enough for the panther population to increase to about 500 animals. At that point, the panther could be removed from the endangered list and allowed to roam free in a protected, suitable habitat within its former range.

Dr. Robert Lacy is a genetics consultant in the effort to save the Florida panther. One of the tools he uses is computer modeling. This is a way of predicting whether the population will grow, decrease, or remain stable, and what inbreeding problems may arise. A variety of information on existing populations is fed into computers. The data includes the ratio of females to males, the number of breeding-age animals in the population, birth rates, and death rates. Computer modeling is a relatively new technique for predicting the future and for offering management options to scientists involved in rescue efforts.

Red and Gray Wolves _____

The red wolf is a shy animal that once roamed a wide area in the eastern and southeastern areas of the United States. Red wolves are shorthaired, and light tan to black in color. They weigh an average of 60 pounds. They are distinguished by high pointed ears, like those of German shepherds, and a long snout. There may be as many as 12 young in a litter, but most become infected with hookworm, a parasite that lives in its host's intestine. Infected pups usually die.

Because people often considered it an enemy, and because the marshes and forests where it leads its secretive life were being destroyed, the red wolf was on the brink of extinction by the 1970s. Oil refineries were polluting the wolves' habitat, and ranchers sometimes shot them. The remaining wolves were confined to several small marshy areas on the coasts of Louisiana and Texas. They were mating with coyotes, probably because the wolf population was so low. There were only 17 purebred red wolves left. They were vulnerable to disease because inbreeding had weakened their immune systems.

In 1973, shortly after Congress passed the Endangered Species Act, the U.S. Fish and Wildlife Service began a program to save the red wolf. It was felt that if the wolves were left in the wild, they would become extinct. All the animals known to be alive were captured and sent to the Tacoma Zoo in Washington State. Slowly the captive wolves began to breed.

When it was time to find a place to reintroduce the wolves to the wild, the U.S. Fish and Wildlife Service found that many hunters and ranchers opposed the plan. After much searching, an area was finally found. It was a boggy section of North Carolina's Outer Banks called the Alligator River National Wildlife Refuge. Wolves were first released there in 1987.

The red wolf's range once extended from Georgia and Florida westward to central Texas and Oklahoma.

The wolves to be released were fitted with radio telemetry collars. They were closely monitored after their release by a team of biologists. At first there was a great deal of worry that the wolves were too used to people and would leave the boundaries of the refuge to enter the communities nearby. The death rate due to disease and accidents was high at first, but eventually the animals seemed to adapt to their new home. The people around the refuge began to adapt to the presence of the wolves, as well. In 1991, the project was declared a success and plans were being drawn for reintroducing the red wolf to Great Smoky Mountains National Park. By 1995, the red wolf population had increased to about 275 animals.

A related scheme involves the reintroduction of the gray wolf to Yellowstone National Park. The gray wolf, also known as the timber wolf, once roamed over the North American continent from Mexico to the Arctic Circle. It is larger than the red wolf, weighing 100 pounds on the average. Gray wolves have shorter snouts and thicker fur, and their ears are wedge-shaped. They live in packs of about 10, and they cooperate in killing larger animals.

By the mid-1950s, nearly two million gray wolves had been slaughtered because people thought they preyed on cattle and attacked humans. Actually, gray wolves prefer to run away from people. In 1994, the gray wolf was found in sizable numbers only in western Canada, Alaska, and northern Minnesota.

In 1995, the U.S. Department of the Interior began reintroducing the gray wolf to Yellowstone National Park and the Frank Church River-of-No-Return Wilderness in Idaho. The plan called for 30 wolves to be taken from Canada and released

Complex greeting behaviors help to maintain the social order in gray wolf packs.

in their new homes each year for the next five years. Once they are established, the wolves will be removed from the endangered list in the Yellowstone and Idaho areas. A fund has been set up from which ranchers are paid for any loss of livestock attributed to wolves.

Why bring the gray wolf back to these areas? The basic reason is that it plays a crucial role in the balance of nature within its ecosystem. Wolves prey on moose, elk, and deer, usually killing the weakest animals—the old, the sick, and some of the young. This helps keep the herds healthy, and it also keeps their populations stable. Too many elk or moose or deer could denude the land, bringing starvation to entire herds. This would, in turn, leave the wolves with little to eat. To remain in balance, nature requires both prey and predator. They keep each other in check and ensure the stability of the ecosystem.

The California Condor

An exciting and controversial reintroduction scheme in the United States involves one of the world's largest birds, the California condor. With its 10-foot wingspan, the condor is an impressive bird. It is able to soar majestically over vast distances as it catches the currents of warm air that spiral up the slopes of mountains. Like other kinds of vultures, condors help to keep the environment clean by feeding on the bodies of dead animals.

Although they were never numerous, condors once ranged up and down the western coast of North America. They were frequently reported by early European travelers, and they are still sacred to the Chumash and other Native American tribes of the West Coast. But these imposing birds gradually began to disappear. In the 1930s, there were about 100 birds. By 1980, just 25 to 30 remained. The U.S. Fish and Wildlife Service was

The California condor is the largest vulture in North America.

called in to solve the mystery of the decline of the condor and to try to save the species.

Noel Snyder, an expert on rescuing endangered species, was put in charge of the project. Since scientists knew little about the bird's nesting and feeding behavior, Snyder and the other members of his team began to track some of the condors with tiny radio transmitters they had attached to the birds' wings. While the scientists tracked the birds, they made plans to capture other condors and bring them to zoos to begin a captive breeding program. Snyder thought the best plan would be to take eggs from condor nests high in the mountains and hatch them in incubators. Most birds will "double-clutch," or lay a second clutch of eggs, if the first is lost. In the wild, condors lay only one egg every other year. Double-clutching would result in many more young condors.

Concerned people raised loud objections to Snyder's plan. Some members of conservation groups felt the plan would make the plight of the condor worse, not better. Carl Koford, who did the first scientific studies of the condor, believed the birds are very sensitive and would not respond well to captivity. Others felt that captive-raised birds would never adjust to life in the wild. The plan turned into a political controversy. Finally the decision was left up to the Fish and Wildlife Service, who decided to follow Snyder's recommendations.

Unfortunately, not long after the plan to collect condor eggs was put into effect, a wild condor chick accidentally died from stress while it was being weighed and measured by field biologists. The public outcry was so loud that the California Fish and Game Commission decided to ban the handling of condors. The condor population, however, continued to decline. In 1983, it was down to only 21 birds. The commission gave permission to restart the radio tracking and captive breeding program. More eggs were collected and successfully hatched at the San Diego Zoo. The parent birds responded by double-clutching.

Meanwhile, the radio telemetry project was providing new information about the condors. Trackers located and recovered the body of a dead condor, and when an autopsy was performed it was found that the bird had died of lead poisoning. This was the first clue to one of the major reasons for the condors' decline. Apparently they had been eating the remains of deer carcasses shot by hunters. The carcasses contained pieces of lead bullets, which poisoned the birds.

People were intruding into the condors' habitat, and with this intrusion came other dangers. Some condors were shot by hunters or by misinformed ranchers who thought condors were killing their livestock. Others were electrocuted when they flew into power lines. By 1985, only nine condors could be found in the wild. The condors were on the very edge of extinction. Snyder began to push for the capture of all the remaining birds. He believed every condor would have to be brought in until a way could be found to keep them safe in the wild.

Once again, political controversy erupted as environmental activists opposed the capture of the last condors. They feared the project would hinder the ongoing fight to preserve condor habitat in the mountains of southern California. They pointed out that it is impossible for condor parents in a captive breeding program to pass on hunting knowledge and other behaviors to their offspring.

The battle between the opposing viewpoints raged on in the courts. By the time Snyder's plan was finally approved, he had had enough of the quarreling and bureaucratic confusion. He had quit the project to work with endangered parrots in Arizona. Mike Wallace, the wildlife ecologist who had been managing the condor programs in the Los Angeles and San Diego zoos, took over.

Not long afterward, all the remaining wild condors were captured and the breeding program was set in motion. Luckily, condors breed easily in captivity—the double-clutching technique encourages them to nest two or three times a season. Eight chicks hatched in 1990, and 13 more in 1991. The breeders were very careful in raising the chicks. They didn't want them to get used to being fed by humans, so at feeding time they hid behind a one-way mirror and used puppets that looked like the head of an adult condor to pass food to the chicks.

With the success of the breeding program assured, it was time for the reintroduction of condors into the wilds of the southern California mountains. First, Wallace and his team held a practice run. They released two female Andean condors,

Condors spend their days soaring high above the ground, watching for carrion.

which are native to South America but are very similar to California condors. When these birds were seen to do well, they were recaptured. It was time to try again, this time with their North American relatives.

Two young California condors, along with two Andean condors for company, were brought to a nest box high on a ridge in the Sespe Sanctuary, a protected area within the Los Padres National Forest in southern California. They were allowed to see their new home, but a net prevented them from flying off prematurely. On January 14, 1992, the net was removed. One by one, the young birds took a brief flight from their nest. Soon all four birds were soaring over the mountains, riding the thermal air currents.

Although the young condors seemed to do well at first, the Sespe Sanctuary proved to be too close to civilization. Some of the condors died after flying into power lines. Others showed a dangerous curiosity about human activities and were seen in nearby towns. One was shot by a picnicker. A new, more remote area of Los Padres National Forest was chosen. Six more birds were released, leaving more than 65 still in zoos.

The captive breeding program has surpassed the expectations of the people involved in it. More than 100 condors had been raised by 1995. The release program has not been as successful. All of the 19 birds released before 1995 died or had to be recaptured for their own safety.

To improve the chances that captive-bred condors yet to be released will survive, they have been placed in a training program to learn to fear humans and structures such as power lines. In February 1995, six condors, the first graduates of this training, were released. They were soon followed by another eight birds. The scientists are optimistic that these birds will survive. A total of 20 condors were to be released by the end of 1996, and the program may be expanded to include a release site in northern California.

The long-range recovery plan calls for 150 birds to be released in the Los Padres National Forest, and a second group of 150 to be released in the Grand Canyon area of Arizona, which is also prime condor habitat. Two widely separated locations were chosen to lessen the risk that the entire population might be wiped out if there were an outbreak of disease. The fate of the condor still hangs in the balance, but there is some hope that this majestic bird will survive.

Whether the captive breeding and release to the wild of endangered species will be a long-term success remains to be seen. Results from some of the projects have been encouraging. There are definitely some animals still alive that would have been extinct without these efforts. However, people must continue to work hard to preserve the remaining natural wildlife habitats.

The Antioch Dunes primrose is one of the world's many endangered plant species.

Chapter Seven

THE WEB OF LIFE

One measure of the success zoos are having in helping endangered animals is the number of young born in captivity. Another is the number of rare species, such as the black-footed ferret, the Arabian oryx, and the golden lion tamarin, that have been returned to nature.

But this is just the beginning. The preservation of large ecosystems is even more important to retaining the earth's biodiversity. These ecosystems are home to hundreds of thousands of species, from large mammals to tiny creatures such as insects and mites.

Many organizations in addition to zoos are working to protect ecosystems and to stop the mismanagement of our planet. The Sierra Club, the Defenders of Wildlife, the World Wildlife Fund, and the Nature Conservancy, among others, work actively to increase the public's awareness of the importance of healthy ecosystems.

Not only does a healthy ecosystem ensure biodiversity, but people reap many benefits from the natural world. Nearly 40 percent of the healing drugs we use are derived from plants, animals, and small organisms. Curare, a poison obtained from plants that grow in the rain forest, is used by surgeons to relax muscles during surgery. An extract from the rosy periwinkle plant that grows in the forests of Madagascar is used to fight leukemia. Cyclosporine, which comes from a fungus that was discovered in Norway, is used to prevent the body from rejecting transplanted organs. Other beneficial natural substances are found every year.

We don't know how many other animals and plants have properties that could be useful to us in the future. Native peoples have used plants to cure diseases for thousands of years. These natural medicines are being studied by researchers who hope to benefit future generations.

These are just some of the gifts nature gives us. Tiny life-forms help to make soil fertile by breaking down organic matter and releasing nutrients. The immense tropical forests influence the climate of the earth by returning moisture to the earth, absorbing carbon dioxide, and releasing oxygen. Scientists are developing new varieties of crops by crossing disease-resistant wild strains with domestic ones.

We haven't identified all the species on earth, much less studied them. It seems sensible to preserve as much as possible of the earth's natural ecological diversity on the chance that many unknown species could be beneficial to us in the future. The rich diversity of our planet may be our most valuable and least appreciated resource.

Humans have evolved over millions of years as part of the natural environment. We have depended on this environment for our survival. Out of this relationship has come an appreciation of the beauty of nature and the rich diversity of life it contains. Primitive peoples delighted in the wildlife they saw around them and drew pictures to express their enjoyment and fascination. Today we bring nature into our homes in the form of plants, flowers, and pets. When we go to the wilderness to find peace and refresh our souls, it's like going back to our roots.

A growing number of people believe that since we are the most powerful and most intelligent of living things, we are responsible for protecting and taking care of all life. It's clear that our efforts in the next 50 years to reverse humanity's destructive ways will be critical.

The zoos are doing their part with their conservation programs. But even if we keep animals alive in zoos, the animals will remain nothing more than refugees. If they have no habitat to go to, all our work will have been for nothing. Only a small percentage of the animals that are bred in captivity are being reintroduced to the wild. To increase the number being let out of the arks, more of our efforts must be aimed at preserving the wilderness and returning to health what we have despoiled in the past.

The Missing Link

Let's go back to the island of Mauritius, where the dodo made its home until its existence was snuffed out by thoughtless humans. People who live on the island noticed that the _Calvaria,_ one of their prized trees, was in danger. All they could find were some very old trees. No young ones were growing anywhere, and when people tried to start new plants from _Calvaria_ seeds, they were unsuccessful.

Scientists were invited to look into the problem. They guessed that the seeds of the _Calvaria_ probably had to pass through the gut of an animal before they could germinate, or sprout. This first step is common to many species of tropical trees. The animals not only help to disperse the seeds, but the chemicals in their stomachs trigger the seeds' germination. But there was no animal on the island that could swallow the large seeds of this tree.

As scientists thought about the problem, they realized that the youngest *Calvaria* trees on Mauritius were about 300 years old. It occurred to them that the dodo had become extinct from the island about 300 years before. Could the dodo have been the missing link in the germination chain?

Since the dodo did not exist anymore, the scientists had to make do with the next best thing. The living bird that most closely resembles the dodo is the domestic turkey, so *Calvaria* seeds were fed to turkeys. To the great joy of the island's inhabitants, who had been afraid they were about to lose another part of their natural heritage, the seeds sprouted.

Life is a wondrous web, with threads of millions of plants and animals woven together in an intricate pattern. Pull one of the threads and the natural balance and harmony of the whole begins to unravel. Humanity may believe it holds the most important place in this web. But the truth is that humans make up nothing more than a single part of the whole.

Ultimately, success in keeping the web of life together depends on everyone. Each of us in his or her own way can support the efforts zoos and conservation organizations are making to help endangered species survive and to protect and restore the animals' natural habitats. If we each do our part, no other animal need suffer the fate of the dodo.

Major Conservation Organizations

The groups listed below are among those working to help wildlife and preserve the environment. You may want to contact them for further information about how you can help endangered wildlife.

African Wildlife Foundation, 1717 Massachusetts Avenue NW, Washington, DC 20036

American Zoo and Aquarium Association, 7970-D Old Georgetown Road, Bethesda, MD 20814

Defenders of Wildlife, 1244 19th Street NW Suite 500, Washington, DC 20036

Environmental Defense Fund, 257 Park Avenue South, New York, NY 10010

Greenpeace U.S.A., 1436 U Street NW, Washington, DC 20009

National Audubon Society, 950 3rd Avenue, New York, NY 10022

National Parks and Conservation Association, 1015 31st Street NW, Washington, DC 20007

National Wildlife Federation, 1400 16th Street NW, Washington, DC 20036

The Nature Conservancy, 1815 North Lynn Street, Arlington, VA 22209

Rainforest Action Network, 466 Green Street, San Francisco, CA 94133

Sierra Club, 730 Polk Street, San Francisco, CA 94109

Wildlife Conservation International, New York Zoological Society, Bronx, NY 10460

Wildlife Preservation Trust International, 34th Street and Girard Avenue, Philadelphia, PA 19104

World Wildlife Fund, U.S.A., 1250 24th Street NW, Washington, DC 20037

GLOSSARY

allele—a particular version of a gene. For example, a plant's gene for seed shape may have an allele for smooth seeds and an allele for wrinkled seeds.

artificial insemination—collecting sperm from a male and inserting it into a female's reproductive tract in order to fertilize her eggs

biodiversity—the variety of different species of plants and animals found in an environment

chromosomes—microscopic threadlike structures that are found in the nucleus of each plant or animal cell. They contain DNA, which is the basic material of heredity.

cloning—a technique for producing genetically identical copies of a living organism

clutch—a nest of eggs

conservation—careful management and protection of a natural resource

crossbreeding—the mating of individuals from different subspecies or breeds of the same species

cryopreservation—storing sperm, eggs, embryos, tissue, or seeds in extremely cold temperatures, usually in liquid nitrogen, for future use in breeding

curator—a person who manages a certain part of a zoo's animal collection, such as mammals, birds, or reptiles

DNA (deoxyribonucleic acid)—the long, twisted molecule in a cell's chromosomes that contains the genetic information that is passed from parents to their young

ecology—the branch of science that studies the interrelationship of living things and their environment

ecosystem—an interdependent community of plants and animals and their environment

ecotourism—a special kind of tourism that allows people to visit and learn about ecologically sensitive areas and the wildlife found in them

embryo—the first stage of growth of a plant or animal. An animal embryo develops from a fertilized egg.

endangered—in danger of becoming extinct

estrus—the period during which a female mammal is fertile and willing to mate. Estrus occurs in a cycle that is different for each species.

extinct—no longer living

fertile—capable of producing offspring

gene—a segment of DNA that is the basic unit of heredity. Each gene provides coded instructions for one or more hereditary traits. A particular trait may be determined by one or by many genes.

gene pool—the collection of all the genes found in all the individuals of a species

genetics—the study of the laws of heredity

gestation—the period of time during which a female mammal carries young in her uterus

habitat—the environment in which a particular kind of animal normally lives and grows

inbreeding—the mating of closely related animals

in vitro fertilization—fertilization of an egg that has been removed from a female animal

nucleus—a structure located near the center of a plant or animal cell. The nucleus contains the cell's hereditary material.

poacher—a person who illegally kills or captures wild animals

primate—any member of the group of mammals that includes humans, apes, monkeys, and lemurs

A two-toed sloth lounges in its enclosure at Omaha's Henry Doorly Zoo.

Ringtailed lemurs live in troops of as many as 30 animals.

silverback—an adult male gorilla that has gray or whitish hair on his back

species—a group of living things that share many common traits. Each species is different from every other species in one or more ways. Members of the same species can breed with each other, and the offspring grow up to look much like their parents.

studbook—a book containing information about the ancestry and reproductive history of animals that are part of a breeding program

surrogate mother—a female that gives birth to the offspring of another female

telemetry—measuring distances or obtaining information by sending and receiving radio signals

uterus—the organ of a female mammal in which the embryo develops

Metric Conversion Factors

When you know	multiply by	to find
inches	2.5	centimeters
feet	0.30	meters
acres	0.40	hectares
pounds	0.45	kilograms
gallons	3.8	liters
°Fahrenheit	0.56 (*after* subtracting 32)	°Celsius

FOR FURTHER READING

Arnold, Caroline. *Saving the Peregrine Falcon*. Minneapolis: Carolrhoda Books, 1985.

Burt, Olive W. *Rescued! America's Endangered Wildlife on the Comeback Trail*. New York: Julian Messner, 1980.

Cajacob, Thomas, and Teresa Burton. *Close to the Wild: Siberian Tigers in a Zoo*. Minneapolis: Carolrhoda Books, 1986.

Casey, Denise. *Black-Footed Ferret*. New York: Dodd, Mead and Company, 1985.

Hoff, Mary, and Mary M. Rodgers. *Our Endangered Planet: Life on Land*. Minneapolis: Lerner Publications, 1992.

Koebner, Linda. *Zoo Book: The Evolution of Wildlife Conservation Centers*. New York: Tom Doherty Associates, 1994.

Lean, Nina. *And Then There Were None—America's Vanishing Wildlife*. New York: Holt, Rinehart and Winston, 1973.

Liptak, Karen. *Saving Our Wetlands and Their Wildlife*. New York: Franklin Watts, 1991.

Mutel, Cornelia F., and Mary M. Rodgers. *Our Endangered Planet: Tropical Rain Forests*. Minneapolis: Lerner Publications, 1991.

Silverberg, Robert. *The Auk, the Dodo, and the Oryx*. New York: Crowell, 1967.

Thane, Maynard. *Endangered Animal Babies: Saving Species One Birth at a Time*. New York: Franklin Watts, 1992.

Wexo, John Bonneth. *Endangered Animals*. San Diego: Wildlife Education, Ltd., 1983.

Wolkomir, Joyce Rogers and Richard Wolkomir. *Junkyard Bandicoots and Other Tales of the World's Endangered Species*. New York: John Wiley and Sons, 1992.

INDEX

Pages listed in **bold** *type refer to photographs.*

alleles. *See* genes
American Zoo and Aquarium
    Association (AZA), 35–36. *See also*
    Species Survival Plans
artificial insemination, 52
aye-aye, 80–81

balance of nature, 94. *See also*
    ecosystems
birds, determining sex of, 58–59
biodiversity. *See* ecosystems
bioparks, 46–47
bongo, **50**, 51–52
breeding programs, and habitat
    preferences, 43–44; and social
    preferences, 42–43; criticism of,
    45–46; limitations on, 45; selection
    of animals for, 34–36; design of,
    44–45. *See also* Center for
    Reproduction of Endangered
    Wildlife, International Species
    Information System, Jersey Wildlife
    Preservation Trust, Species Survival
    Plans

Center for Reproduction of
    Endangered Wildlife (CREW),
    51–52; CREW International,
    61–63; facilities, 55; research at,
    56–57
cheetah, **39**, 46, 48
chimpanzee, 28–29, 43, 48
cloning, 52–53, 61
condor, California, 94–99; captive
    breeding of, 95–97, 99; lead
    poisoning of, 96; tracking of, 95,
    96; survival training, 99
crane, white-naped, 49, 59

DDT (dichloro-diphenyl-
    trichloroethane), 72, **73**
Dietz, Dr. James, 88

Dietz, Lou Anne, 88–89
DNA (deoxyribonucleic acid), 58–60.
    See also genes
dodo, **6**, 7–9, 103–104
Dresser, Dr. Betsy, 61, 62
Durrell, Gerald, 80

ecosystems, 70–71, 76; and
    introduction of foreign species, 71,
    72; of islands, 71; preservation of,
    101–102. *See also* bioparks
ecotourism, 65–66, 78–79
eland, 51–52, 56
elephant, African, 59–60
elephant, Asian, **40**, 42, 48
embryos, freezing of, 53; splitting of,
    52–53; transfer of, 51–54
Endangered Species Act of 1973,
    74–75. *See also* laws protecting
    animals
environment, damage to, 72–73. *See
    also* habitats, destruction of
extinction, 8, 9; of plants, 72; rate of,
    69–70; reversal of, 63

ferret, black-footed, **10**, 11–21, 48;
    and prairie dog, 11–12, 13, 14, 16;
    captive breeding programs in zoos,
    21; disease and, 14–15, 21; ideal
    population of, 44; release sites, 16,
    21; survival training, 15–19; threats
    to, 12, 13; tracking of, 19–20
Fossey, Dian, 66, 67
freezing of biological material, 53, 63

gaur, 48, 57
genes, 36–40; dominant, 38;
    manipulation of, 60–61; recessive,
    37, 38
genetic diversity, 36–37; and
    population size, 39
genetic engineering, 60–61

genetic fingerprinting. *See* DNA
genetics. *See* genes
gorilla, lowland, **22,** 23–27, 48
gorilla, mountain, 48, **64,** 65–68,
    78–79; civil war and, 68
greenhouse effect, 72–73

habitats, destruction of, 27, **32,** 33,
    40, 66, 68–69; protection of,
    76–82. *See also* environment,
    damage to
Hagenbeck, Karl, 27
horse, Przewalski's, 48, 57
humans, growth of population of, 66,
    68; and benefits from nature,
    101–102

in vitro fertilization, 54
inbreeding, 35, 36, 39; of Florida
    panther, 90; in zoos, 40–41
indicator species, 71
International Species Information
    System (ISIS), 41–42
International Union for the
    Conservation of Nature (IUCN),
    34

Jersey Wildlife Preservation Trust,
    80–81

keystone species, 76
Kleiman, Dr. Devra, 87–88
Koford, Carl, 96

laws protecting animals, 66–68, 72,
    73–75
Leakey, Dr. Louis, 67

oryx, Arabian, 48, 61, 83–85; ideal
    population of, 44
owl, spotted, **70,** 71

panda, giant, 24, 46, 48, 54
panther, Florida, 89–90
pigeon, passenger, 63
poachers, 23, 24, 66–68; tracking of,
    59–60

Red Data Books, 34

Seal, Dr. Ulysses, 41
Snyder, Noel, 95–97
Species Survival Plans (SSP), 40–42;
    list of, 48–49

tamarin, golden lion, 41–42, 48,
    86–89; reintroduction site, 87;
    survival training, 88
tiger, Bengal, 54
tiger, Siberian, 49, 54; ideal
    population of, 44
tracking wild animals, 18, 19–20,
    95–96

Wallace, Mike, 97–98
whales, hunting of, 73
Wildt, Dr. David, 54
wolf, gray, 93–94; and balance of
    nature, 94; reasons for decline of,
    93
wolf, red, **18,** 49, 91–92; threats to,
    91

zoos, and animal behavior, 28–29;
    purpose of, 24–25, 33–35, 46–47;
    redesign of, 24–30; visitors to,
    30–31. *See also* breeding programs

ABOUT THE AUTHORS

Nicholas Nirgiotis was born in Chicago, where he has lived most of his life. He is a graduate of the University of Chicago, and he has worked as a teacher and freelance writer. His interest in conservation has been lifelong. He has traveled widely, both in the United States and abroad, to gain an understanding of the plight of wildlife and to observe the efforts being made by zoos and conservation organizations to stem the tide of extinction. He is the author of several books for children and young adults. When not working, he likes to travel and read.

Theodore Nirgiotis heads the environmental task force of Diablo Valley College (California), where he teaches mathematics. Researching the biodiversity crisis led to co-authoring this book. Mr. Nirgiotis is a graduate of Harvard College, and he served in the Peace Corps, teaching in a remote village in the Fiji Islands. After leaving Fiji, he spent a year traveling in Southeast Asia and India. One of his first encounters with an endangered species was with orangutans on Sumatra. Since then he has traveled to many other parts of the world, witnessing the struggle of a number of species fighting to stay alive, such as the giant leatherback turtles of Malaysia and the mountain gorillas of Rwanda.

PHOTO ACKNOWLEDGMENTS

Photographs © William Muñoz, with the following exceptions: pp. 40, 46, 64, 67, 69, 70, 73, 75, 77, 78, 86 © Gerry Ellis/Ellis Nature Photography; p.6, Minneapolis Athenaeum; p.95, D. Clendenen/USFWS; p.98, J. Grantham/NAS.

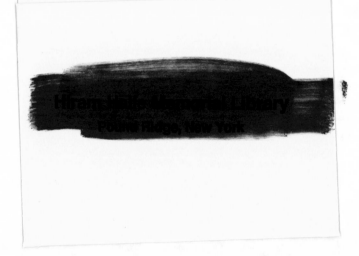